About This Book

Why is this topic important?

Everyone knows that experiential activities are the best tools to engage your participants in training sessions and meetings. But there is a problem: These activities take a long time to design and facilitate. This book provides an elegant solution: Use *jolts* that can be conducted in a few minutes and give a long-lasting wake-up call and powerful insights.

What can you achieve with this book?

This book first provides a rationale for using jolts and a caveat against their abuse. It gives practical guidelines to achieve a variety of results such as capturing participants' attention at the beginning of a session, smoothly transitioning between one training topic (or agenda item) and the next, keeping participants awake and energized after a lunch break, tapping into the wisdom of the group to derive profound insights, and breaking up lengthy lectures and information dumps with relevant activities. In short, the book helps the reader to design, deliver, and debrief engaging jolts.

How is this book organized?

The book is divided into two distinct sections. Part 1 provides a conceptual introduction to jolts and practical guidelines for conducting different types of jolts with different groups of participants. This part also contains a comprehensive why-to and how-to section on debriefing after a jolt to reflect on the activity, derive useful insights, and share them with each other. Part 2 features the bulk of the content in the form of fifty ready-to-use jolts. Each jolt is presented in a standardized format the includes a synopsis, statement of purpose, appropriate training topics, number of participants, time requirement, supplies and equipment, step-by-step instructions for conducing the activity, debriefing questions and suggestions, learning points, variations, and field notes.

About Pfeiffer

Pfeiffer serves the professional development and hands-on resource needs of training and human resource practitioners and gives them products to do their jobs better. We deliver proven ideas and solutions from experts in HR development and HR management, and we offer effective and customizable tools to improve workplace performance. From novice to seasoned professional, Pfeiffer is the source you can trust to make yourself and your organization more successful.

Essential Knowledge Pfeiffer produces insightful, practical, and comprehensive materials on topics that matter the most to training and HR professionals. Our Essential Knowledge resources translate the expertise of seasoned professionals into practical, how-to guidance on critical workplace issues and problems. These resources are supported by case studies, worksheets, and job aids and are frequently supplemented with CD-ROMs, websites, and other means of making the content easier to read, understand, and use.

Essential Tools Pfeiffer's Essential Tools resources save time and expense by offering proven, ready-to-use materials—including exercises, activities, games, instruments, and assessments—for use during a training or team-learning event. These resources are frequently offered in looseleaf or CD-ROM format to facilitate copying and customization of the material.

Pfeiffer also recognizes the remarkable power of new technologies in expanding the reach and effectiveness of training. While e-hype has often created whizbang solutions in search of a problem, we are dedicated to bringing convenience and enhancements to proven training solutions. All our e-tools comply with rigorous functionality standards. The most appropriate technology wrapped around essential content yields the perfect solution for today's on-the-go trainers and human resource professionals.

Pfeiffer
www.pfeiffer.com   *Essential resources for training and HR professionals*

JOLTS!

Activities to Wake Up and Engage Your Participants

Sivasailam "Thiagi" Thiagarajan
Tracy Tagliati

Pfeiffer
A Wiley Imprint
www.pfeiffer.com

Library of Congress Cataloging-in-Publication Data

Thiagarajan, Sivasailam, author.
    Jolts! : Activities to Wake Up and Engage Your Participants / Sivasailam "Thiagi" Thiagarajan, Tracy Tagliati.
      p. cm
    ISBN 978-0-470-90003-1 (pbk.)
      1. Management games. 2. Educational games. 3. Personnel management.   I. Tagliati, Tracy, author.
      II. Title.
HD30.26.T486 2011
658.3'124—dc22

2010045670

Acquiring Editor: Holly J. Allen
Director of Development: Kathleen Dolan Davies
Production Editor: Dawn Kilgore
Editor: Rebecca Taff

Editorial Assistant: Lindsay Morton
Manufacturing Supervisor: Becky Morgan
Printed in the United States of America
Printing 10 9 8 7 6 5 4 3 2 1

In fond memory of our friend
Juliet

Contents

On the Website

Electronic copies of the slides, handouts, and audio recordings for these jolts are provided on the website for this book at:

url: www.pfeiffer.com/go/jolts

password: professional

Slides

Jolt 17—Free Time

Jolt 19—How Many Squares?

Jolt 26—New Word

Jolt 31—Photo Analysis

Jolt 33—Psychic Cards

Jolt 38—Six Tiles

Jolt 39—Stroop

Handouts

Jolt 4—Dear John Handout 1

Jolt 4—Dear John Handout 2

Jolt 4—Dear John Handout 3

Jolt 5—Decode Handout 1

Jolt 5—Decode Handout 2

Jolt 5—Decode Handout 3

Jolt 15—First Touch! Rule Sheet

Jolt 16—Free! Handout

Jolt 18—How Fast? Puzzle

Jolt 18—How Fast? Puzzle

Jolt 20—Last Week Questionnaire 1

Jolt 20—Last Week Questionnaire 2

Jolt 22—Long Words Handout

Jolt 25—Mingle Handout

Jolt 31—Photo Analysis Handout 1

Jolt 31—Photo Analysis Handout 2

Jolt 35—Scrambled Words Handout

Jolt 36—Sequencing, Memory Test Handout 1

Jolt 36—Sequencing, Memory Test Handout 2

Jolt 41—Team Planning Handout: How to Solve Micro-Sudoku Puzzles

Jolt 42—Team Power Handout 1

Jolt 42—Team Power Puzzles Solutions

Preface

Thiagi designed his first training game (for a high school physics lesson on internal combustion engines) in 1960, long before his co-author Tracy was born. Since then Thiagi has developed hundreds of different types of games, simulations, and learning activities, and this passion has defined his career. His love for and belief in the power of experiential learning has made him a sought after teacher who travels the world sharing his knowledge with other designers and trainers. In fact, Thiagi may hold the record for game design; he has made a point to design a new training game each day since 1998. Ever mindful of changing times (and perhaps because of his younger colleagues with low attention spans), Thiagi has been compressing the time requirements for his learning activities over the last ten years and focused his inspiration on the design and use of jolts, the subject of this book.

Tracy joined the Thiagi gamesters after spending her developmental years as a global nomad, finally settling in California and teaching vocational education to young adults. After a stint in the corporate training world (first at a franchise of Crestcom International and then at Mercury Insurance Group), Tracy joined the Thiagi Group in 2008 and began working with Thiagi co-designing, co-facilitating, and co-authoring jolts. She says her current specialty is arguing with Thiagi.

The jolts presented in this book are field tested. Some of the activities have been featured as part of sessions on designing and using jolts at professional conferences such as the American Society for Training and Development (ASTD), the International Alliance for Learning (IAL), the International Society for Performance Improvement (ISPI), and the North American Simulation and Gaming Association (NASAGA). Jointly and separately, we have incorporated jolts in our training workshops around the world from Cape Town to Chennai, from Johannesburg to Paris, from Singapore and Sydney and Zurich to Rancho Cucamonga.

In every session and in every country we have visited, jolts have enabled us to achieve two valuable outcomes: We have kept our participants engaged in the learning and provided them with useful and sometimes profound insights (no matter the native culture or background of the participants).

The step-by-step procedures and supporting principles outlined in this book put the power of experiential learning in your hands and as a result the potential to create a more engaged, energized, and high performing workforce.

Sivasailam "Thiagi" Thiagarajan
Bloomington, Indiana
thiagi@thiagi.com

Tracy Tagliati
Thousand Oaks, California
tracy@thiagi.com

Acknowledgments

Many people have contributed to the development of jolts by funding design projects, participating in our training workshops, providing constructive feedback, sharing conceptual frameworks, and making sarcastic remarks. We want to thank all of the folks (listed below in alphabetical order by their first names) for their significant contributions:

Alain Rostain, Andrew Boyarsky, April Davis, Bernie DeKoven, Bill Matthews, Bob Wiele, Brandon Carson, Brent Travers, Brian Remer, Brittany Corbucci, Bruno Hourst, Carl Binder, Chris Saeger, Chuck Adams, Clark Aldrich, Curtis Bonk, Darlene Van Tiem, Darryl Sink, David Gouthro, Debbie Newman, Diane Dormant, Donna Marks, Eileen Orth, Ellen S. Kay Gehrke, Ethan Sanders, Eva Martony, Frances Kemmerer, Gareth Kingston, Gary Travers, Gary VanAntwerp, George Koehn, Glenn Parker, Guy Wallace, Heather Robinson, Jane Sink, Jason England Thiagarajan, Jeff Lefton, Jin Abe, John Walber, Jonathan Finklestein, Judith Blohm, Julie England, Julie Groshens, Karen Stoeller, Kat Koppett, Kay Travers, Ken Bellemare, Kurt Squire, Larry Lipman, Laura Mankowski, Leah Nelson, Les Lauber, Lindsay Robinson, Liza Tagliati, Lucy Chaddha, Lucy Thiagarajn, Luella Hobson, Lynn Kearney, Marc Shiman, Mario Tagliati, Mark Giganti, Mark Isabella, Mark Marrow, Marla Schwartz, Marty Cielens, Matt Richter, Michelle Primack, Nigel Bailey, Patrick Dorpmund, Paul Butler, Paul Cook, Peter Bechtel, Pieter van der Hijden, Raja Thiagarajan, Ray Jiminez, RC Palan, Rebecca Saeger, Regina Rowland, Richard Pearlstein, Rod Travers, Roger Greenaway, Samuel van den Bergh, Sandy Fowler, Sharon Bowman, Stannis Benjamin, Steve Sugar, Tanya Koivisto, Tim Scudder, Will Thalheimer, William Wake, and Willy Kriz.

PART 1
What Jolts Are and How to Use Them

Chapter 1
What Are Jolts and How Can I Use Them?

As the definition of the word implies, *Jolts* are brief activities that challenge (and maybe push, jar, and sometimes shock) participants to re-examine their comfortable assumptions and habitual practices (see definition below).

Jolt

1 to cause to move with a sudden jerky motion
2 to give a knock or blow to; specifically: to jar with a quick or hard blow
3 a: to disturb the composure of: shock; b: to interfere with roughly, abruptly, and disconcertingly

---

While not directly aimed at skill building, the fifty *Jolts* we describe in this book are nonetheless powerful training tools that will help you engage your participants and focus attention on your learning event. In addition, *Jolts* are perfectly suited for use in many types of training interventions, including training in diversity, sexual harassment, change management, customer focus, and creative problem solving. Here are a few other suggestions on how to use these activities. You may use *Jolts* to

- Capture participants' attention at the beginning of a session
- Segue between one training topic and the next
- Keep participants awake and energized after a lunch break
- Make a profound, thought-provoking point at the end of another activity (for example, to demonstrate the difficulty of making changes in behaviors and habits)
- Vary the pace and break up lengthy presentations such as presentations of technical content
- Anchor a lecture by choosing an appropriate *jolt* that will allow you to present your content as part of the *jolt* debriefing
- Illustrate effective learning techniques or emphasize the importance of follow-up activities

Conducting Jolts

Skilled facilitation is essential to the success of jolts since some of these activities require participants to examine differences between people and cultures as well as preconceived notions connected directly to potential emotion "hot buttons" issues. Other activities are simply fast paced and highly competitive so keeping emotions in check requires the finesse of an experienced facilitator. This is particularly true during the debrief portion (see Chapter 6) of the activity when strong emotions or negative reactions often surface. That is why we offer specific detailed instructions and appropriate warnings about the use of these exercises.

In the next chapter you will find a scenario of a jolt exercise that will be useful to your full understanding of jolts. But first you'll need the grounding provided by the rest of this chapter so that the principles are clearly understood.

The Types and Categories of Jolts

Jolts are broadly classified into two categories, *entrapment* jolts and *enlightenment* jolts. As you might imagine, both types present unique facilitation challenges. Jolts are designed to be used with individual participants or groups and either nudge, push, or perhaps force participants to consider new ways to thinking or behaving, thus our cautions about use and the careful instructions provided in this book. We have designed the jolts to employ a variety of media prompts that increase the effectiveness of the jolts, including the use of printed cards and audio and video clips. Some of the jolts do require simple props for successful execution, but we have deliberately limited the number of jolts requiring props to simplify facilitation. Finally, we vary the required tasks to take advantage of a wide range of individual preferences and learner types. You will find exercises involving listening and thinking, listening and remembering, and listening and talking as well as drawing, negotiating, and performing physical activities.

The Art of a Jolt

Clearly, using jolts is fun, energizing, and highly effective in many training situations. But before using them, you need to carefully consider both your motivation for using them and your ability to handle difficult situations.

Chapter 5 provides some very specific recommendations, but in general we suggest the judicious use of these jolts. When you do use a jolt, we highly recommend setting aside plenty of time for debriefing. In addition, we suggest a nimble, flexible approach to facilitation that includes a rapid pace when conducting jolts and a willingness to abandon a chosen jolt if you anticipate a too severe reaction from participants or if a point has been made sufficiently before the end of a jolt.

Debriefing a Jolt

Without a debriefing discussion, jolts would certainly not be an effective training, learning, or engagement tool; in fact, jolts might even be considered potentially harmful without careful debriefing. Chapter 6 offers you detailed instructions on how to debrief jolts, but in general there are three reasons to support our insistence on debriefing:

1. More learning results from *reflecting* on an experience than from the experience itself.
2. Debriefing reduces possible negative impact from a jolt by allowing "wind down" time and increasing opportunities for positive insights.
3. Debriefing maximizes impact and connection to your training objectives.

Some activities benefit more than others from extensive debriefing, and you will find more guidance in Chapter 6. However, you can be sure that jolts with potential strong positive or negative emotional reactions or activities that are too brief or abstract to be understood without a debriefing are clear-cut candidates for this follow-up session.

Next Steps

Now that you have an overview of what a jolt is and how to use it, perhaps *showing you* rather than *telling* you how to introduce and facilitate a jolt session might be the best next step. Chapter 2 is intended as your window into how an experienced facilitator might handle a typical jolt session. If reading through the provided scenario is not enough *showing* for you, then go to our website (www.thiagi.com) and click on the jolt icon on our home page. You will find links to a few jolt session that clearly demonstrate the ropes of successful jolt facilitation. In addition, the website offers you some additional jolt-related content for both novice and advanced facilitators.

Chapter 2
Story of a Jolt

In the previous chapter you learned the basics of jolts along with how and when to use these powerful and sometimes provocative activities. Now, as promised, we offer a detailed narrative to convey what it is like to conduct a jolt in a training session. The narrative is written from the participant's point of view so that you fully understand the need for careful execution, facilitation, and debriefing of the jolt. As noted in Chapter 1, if you would like to watch an actual jolt in action, go to www.thiagi.com, click on the Jolts icon, and follow the links provided.

Personal Productivity Workshop

You are on your way to attend a workshop in the company's new training facility. Your HR department has touted the program you are about to attend on improving productivity and managing multiple projects as innovative, practical, and perhaps even inspiring. Although you are looking forward to discovering any new information, tips, or techniques the workshop may reveal, the idea of abandoning all that work on your desk, even if it is only to attend a half-day workshop, has increased your anxiety.

For weeks, you have battled an energy-draining inertia of unknown origin. Lately, you've attacked the issue head on. You've left your home every morning determined to get more done, to be more efficient, to get off the dime; but every day you come home utterly disappointed about your ability to affect any significant change. You are worried that your supervisor will stop by for a friendly chat or perhaps to check on the status of other assignments. You play out the familiar scenario in your mind, the one in which your supervisor makes a humorous remark about the disorganized stacks of files on your desk and the annoyingly supportive follow-up email asking if you would like to attend an organization training class very similar to the one you are on your way to attend.

After taking your customary seat near the back of the room, the facilitator, Marie, walks in at 8:20 a.m. (right on time) and starts the workshop. Without any preliminary comments or introductions about the workshop, she begins the program.

"Good morning everyone," Marie says brightly over all the chatter and chuckles produced by the group of colleagues and friends. When Marie feels she has everyone's attention she begins.

"Okay, here's what I want you to do to start today's training. I want everyone to put their hands together and clap just once." Most participants (including you) are caught by surprise and a bit confused. But you and the other attendees attempt to carry out Marie's instructions. The resulting group clap was more a smattering of individual claps along with a generous portion of chuckles and guffaws and class clown comments.

Marie smiles at the group and comments about the group's performance. "That was way too ragged," she says. "So why don't we try it again?"

"This time," Marie continues, "I'd like everyone to clap just once in total synchrony so that our collective clap will sound like a single, loud clap. Do you think that's possible?"

You are beginning to wonder what this exercise has to do with personal productivity, but decide to play along for now.

"I know that this may be difficult for some of you," Marie says, "so I am going to provide you with a non-electronic performance support system you will all recognize." Marie waits two beats and then delivers the punch line. "I am going to count to three." Despite yourself, you chuckle and feel yourself relax a bit. Although Marie has given the complete instructions, she asks again if everyone understands and repeats them once more, this time even more slowly and deliberately:

"OK," she says, "Here are the instructions—I am going to count to three [she counts, holding up a finger for each count] and I want everyone to clap together when I say [she emphasizes the word] *clap*!"

You nod your head in agreement along with the rest of the group and raise your hands in front of you, poised to clap your hands together when prompted by Marie.

One, Two, Three

Marie surveys the room to make sure everyone is paying attention. She raises her hands in front of her and holds them a few inches apart. Then she breathes slightly before saying the words, "One, two, three." When she says "three," Marie claps her hands decisively.

All the participants in the room follow her lead and clap their hands in unison. After a short pause, Marie says the word, "clap" and you almost immediately get the joke. You feel a little embarrassed and a bit annoyed. You feel the facilitator trapped you into making a mistake and now the anxiety caused by your overzealous supervisor and backlog of the paperwork is back. You wonder whether you could slip out of the class now and maybe make some progress on those reports before the dreaded email arrives. At least you'd be able to defend yourself.

Sorry About That

While the participants laugh and look around the room to make sure that everyone made the same mistake and to ensure they have not been singled out as the "class dope," Marie apologizes for deception and for trapping everyone to make a mistake. Then the affable facilitator explains to the group why the activity has a serious point to make.

"You see," Marie says, "this exercise is a dramatic example of the gap between *understanding* and *application*. Everyone heard and thought they understood that they were supposed to wait until I said the word 'Clap' before actually clapping their hands together. Yet no one applied this knowledge."

"So what's the point?" Marie continued, "The point is this: It is not sufficient for you to merely understand the principles we will explore in the workshop. Rather, it is the *application* that will determine how successfully we have spent our time here together."

You feel a little better now that you understand the point of the exercise, but from now on you determine to listen carefully, especially if today's workshop includes any more traps like this one.

So This Is a Jolt

The example provided above is a simple (and pretty mild) jolt and it is included in the book as Jolt 40, Synchronized Clapping. Despite its simplicity, this jolt includes all the classic elements of this type of experiential activity:

- **Time-Limited.** Jolts last for a very short period of time. Marie's jolt lasted for a minute and half. Some jolts may last for less than a minute. By our definition, no jolt can last more than five minutes.
- **Insight- Rather Than Skills-Focused.** Jolts provide participants with insights rather than skills. They startle the participants into re-examining their assumptions and revising their habitual practices.
- **Possibility of Emotional Impact.** Jolts produce emotional effects. Some jolts produce feelings of discomfort or elation; all jolts result in "aha" moments and surprise.
- **Participant Interaction and Introspection.** Some jolts require interaction among participants, and all jolts require *introspection* on the part of individual participants.
- **Debriefing.** The discussion after the activity maximizes the learning outcomes from the jolt. This process involves explanations from the facilitator and discussions among the participants.

Participant Emotional Baggage

In addition to the standard elements noted above, jolts often increase the possibility that the emotional baggage that every participant brings to training events (including anxieties, insecurities, and hot button issues) will not stay safely packed away until the end of the event. In the scenario presented above, the participant with the passive-aggressive boss was primed to have a confrontation. Marie's explanation kept the situation in check. But what if the purpose of the jolt had been to explore what keeps people from taking positive action? Only expert facilitation and debriefing would prevent this participant from publicly venting his anger and frustration. Would you know how to handle such an outburst?

As you will see in Chapter 6, we provide very specific techniques that will help you control and channel the emotional reactions to group activities. Each of the jolts outlined in Part 2 provides specific debriefing techniques.

Now that you understand what a jolt is and how it works, the next three chapters describe the types of jolts, the key ways to conduct jolts, and important tips to successfully facilitate them.

Chapter 3
Types of Jolts

As noted earlier, we classify jolts broadly into two types, *entrapment* jolts and *enlightenment* jolts. This classification—how the jolt is positioned or perceived by the participants—is useful for picking a jolt for a specific training situation or purpose. Further classification of jolts is possible by grouping the activities by shared elements and themes and by the number of participants, media type, or props used, or by the grouping or repetition of jolts. This chapter explores these application and usage variations and offers ways you might customize jolts for your own training needs or situations. Specifically, this chapter covers the following classification categories:

- Positioning
- Number of Participants
- Media and Props
- Activity Type
- Facilitator Methodology

Positioning

How jolts are positioned is perhaps the most useful classification. As we've pointed out, *entrapment* jolts are designed to reveal more effective alternative behaviors to participants after they've been encouraged (or maybe even tricked) into following comfortable, familiar, and practiced behavior patterns. As the name implies, the facilitator takes on a provocative stance when conducting entrapment jolts.

Enlightenment jolts are designed to help participants discover "aha" moments that connect to core principles and the work of reinforcing effective strategies. Your job as an enlightenment jolt facilitator is to be a coach for the participants.

Entrapment Jolts
Part 2 of this book contains several entrapment exercises, including the two examples used below. Many of the activities are designed to lead the participant away from the correct answer or approach and then point out the mistake. For example, in Jolt 26, New Word, participants achieve success in the first round by using a specific strategy. The context of the second round appears to be very similar to that of the first one. However, the strategy from the first round does not work in the second round. In order to succeed

in the second round, participants must use an entirely different strategy. Another entrapment jolt, Jolt 5, Decode, strongly implies competition among teams. However, the winning strategy requires the opposite: collaboration among different teams.

While these "bait and switch" activities are often fun and produce nothing more than good natured laughter, it is easy to see how some participants may not appreciate being "trapped."

Enlightenment Jolts

You will find several enlightenment jolts in Part 2, and all these jolts enable the participants to discover useful strategies and principles. For example, Jolt 28, Next Action, is a thought experiment designed to guide an individual participant through a systematic process of identifying needs, specifying goals, and deciding on a small next step. The participant must complete the task in a limited time frame—a matter of minutes—and can complete the assignment without any challenge or confrontation.

Another enlightenment jolt, Jolt 14, Excited, relies on a larger group of participants to playfully provide stage directions to a smaller group charged with holding up letters that spell a word. Participants discover their moment of *enlightenment* during debriefing when the facilitator helps them identify key factors that contribute to high levels of motivation.

Number of Participants

The second major way to classify jolts is by the number of participants involved. In theory, most of the jolts described in this book are appropriate for use with groups of any size. Some exercises require at least two participants (Jolt 27, Newton), other team-driven jolts (Jolt 1, Alliances; Jolt 23, Me and My Team) require enough participants to form one or two teams. Some jolts such as Jolt 40, Synchronized Clapping, work best in larger groups. However, most jolts presented in this book can be conducted with just a single participant.

Media and Props

Some jolts in this book require the use of PowerPoint slides, while others require that you have access to audio or video recording devices. While most jolts in this book do not require props, some jolts do require at least some facsimile of the required prop. For example, Jolt 33, Psychic Card, uses PowerPoint slides to present playing cards.

If you use Jolt 29, Palm to Palm, then the use of audio recording equipment is recommended. Although not suggested directly in this book, it is possible to incorporate video recording into a jolts activity. If you would like to see how this is done, visit the thiagi.com website and click the jolts tab.

Clearly, trainers and professional facilitators are familiar with the use of props and appreciate their learning impact. We have deliberately chosen to take a simple approach and not require excessive use of props. However, some jolts do require their use. For example, Jolt 49, Workers and Watchers, requires blindfolds and pieces of ropes. Jolt 1, Alliances, requires the use of playing cards while facilitating the jolts. Jolt 9, Double Your Money, and Jolt 6, Dollar Action, require real cash. You will need a puzzle for Jolt 22, Long Words, and Jolt 42, Team Power. Simple pen and paper is needed to successfully run Jolt 7, Don't Lift the Pen, and Jolt 10, Draw a Hand.

Activity Type

Another way to classify jolts is by what the activity requires of the participants. We have broken these activities into the six broad categories listed below and given examples from Part 2:

- Listening and Thinking (Jolt 2, By the Numbers)
- Listening and Remembering (Jolt 24, Memory Test)
- Listening and Talking (Jolt 8, Double Talk)
- Drawing (Jolt 11, Draw a Tree)
- Negotiating (Jolt 1, Alliances)
- Physical Activity (Jolt 21, Limits)

Your use of the jolts described in Part 2 may reveal other more specific categories or perhaps even fewer categories. That's fine and we have no magic agenda other than to help you use jolts to drive learning results.

Facilitator Methodology

As noted in Chapter 1, strong facilitation skills are required to successfully use jolts in your training programs. In addition, facilitators who use jolts must be flexible and comfortable using a wide variety of approaches, including alternate ways of using printed materials and creatively mixing two or more jolts for a specific purpose. This approach is also called *serial jolts*.

Printed Instruction Jolts

Experienced facilitators are very familiar with the use of printed materials to conduct an activity. However, some jolts require little facilitator interaction with the participants. For example, a simple jolt may begin with the facilitator handing out a one-page Sudoku puzzle. In addition to the usual instructions about how to solve a Sudoku puzzle, the handout includes a scoring system that announces the following:

> If you solve the puzzle within 1 minute, you receive 1,000 points;
> If you solve the puzzle within 2 minutes, you receive 500 points;
> If you solve the puzzle within 3 minutes, you receive 200 points;
> If it takes you longer than 3 minutes to solve the puzzle, you receive 0 points.

The puzzle looks tough because only a few numbers are placed in the grid and most participants give up soon after beginning, while a few struggle on valiantly until time is called at the three-minute mark by the facilitator's whistle.

What the participants did not know about the exercise was that not everyone had the same numbers on their Sudoku grids. During the debriefing discussion, the facilitator points out that, had they talked to each other and shared information, the puzzle could have easily be solved within one minute.

The discussion focuses on the tendency to not collaborate with each other unless explicitly directed to do so. The main learning point of this jolt is that if teamwork is the default work mode, then productivity increases and new resources are discovered.

As you gain more experience using jolts, you will discover that different ways to use puzzles to highlight different principles and concepts. However, in most cases you should use puzzle activities to highlight an interpersonal principle such as teamwork, diversity, or competition and collaboration. Otherwise, the activity is simply a puzzle-solving activity with no instructional value.

Serial Jolts

We use the term *serial jolt* to refer to the use of several jolts that are conducted in succession, one after the other. The methodology requires some skill on the facilitator's part to mix and match jolts for an intended purpose. Below are some typical serial jolt scenarios and uses. Note that despite the mixing and matching of jolts, the debriefing activity follows each jolt individually.

- Trusting Assumptions
- Same Principle, Different Context
- Small Changes Matter
- Bite Sized Simulations

Trusting Assumptions

While a single jolt does provide participants with useful insights, it is still sometimes hard to transfer this learning from a single, stand alone jolt to similar real-world situations. You can use the repeated and varied practice of serial jolts to reinforce concepts and thus increase the probability of transfer and application.

For example, Jolt 38, Six Tiles, uses serial jolts to increase participants' awareness of unnecessary assumptions made when solving problems. The first jolt involves displaying six imaginary tiles, each with three letters:

MAN   LES   OBJ   AGE   SON   ECT

Participants are asked to rearrange the tiles so that the result spells out three words. Participants are usually able to solve this problem easily and produce the correct answer:

MANAGE,   LESSON,   OBJECT

Follow-up jolt exercises appear to be the same since all include six tiles of three letters each. However, each successive jolt "traps" the participants into assuming that certain restrictions apply such as all the tiles must be used, the words created must be in English, that the tiles may not be rotated or that each tile may be used only once, or that a space must be used between words. Each failure to solve the tile problem increases the participant's paranoia about the mindless assumptions they are making to solve common problems.

Same Principal, Different Context

This type of serial jolt highlights the idea that a single strategy will not solve every problem and encourages creative, strategic thinking. Here is how a context serial jolt might play out in a classroom.

Begin with the simple Jolt 26, New Word, that is designed to jolt participants into realizing the dangers of falling into ruts. Facilitate the jolt as instructed by first presenting participants with these words:

NEW DEER

Then ask participants to rearrange the seven letters contained in the separate two words into one word. After some serious thinking, most participants are able to find the solution:

RENEWED

For the follow-up jolt, you give the participant these two words followed by the same instructions:

NEW DOOR

Of course, the second jolt is harder to do and most participants give up trying long before the facilitator reveals that the solution ONE WORD does comply with the instructions. After all, the language used in the instructions was "one word" and not "single word." During the debriefing discussion, the facilitator reiterates the point that past strategies are not always appropriate for solving new problems.

Small Changes Matter

This type of serial jolt uses the same basic setup and relies on minor variations to make a point such as how a change in one factor influences people's behaviors and outcomes.

For example, begin your facilitation with Jolt 42, Team Power. The three-minute activity begins with passing out random playing cards to the participants. Then the facilitator asks the group to team up in groups of five to create the best poker hand possible.

The next round begins the same way with handing out random playing cards. However, in this round, you announce that each member of the winning team will receive a $5 cash prize. A third round of this jolt is played the same except that members of the winning team receive different cash prize awards.

As the facilitator, your job is to point out how the introduction of money increases competitive and selfish behaviors.

Bite-Sized Simulations

While lengthy simulations can be effective, sometimes using a series of well-constructed jolts throughout a workshop (along with the debriefing discussion at the end) may increase learning and retention. For example, if a team activity involves planning, implementing, and improving the process, we might divide the process into three related jolts, each ending with an appropriate debriefing discussion.

Final Thoughts and Cautions

The different categories presented in this chapter do not represent every way you might use or customize jolts. For example, we may use a video recording as part of a drawing jolt that encourages creativity. Or we might adjust Jolt 29, Palm to Palm, so that it can be used with two people instead of one. By adjusting the jolt in this way you can create a new entrapment activity that forces two participants (one short and one tall) to behave in predictable ways, that is, the taller person automatically resisting a push against the palm, even though no such instructions were given.

The caveat we offer on the use of entrapment jolts in a series is the possibility of creating high levels of participant frustration. Some participants may even voice this frustration with a comment such as, "We've got the point." If this happens, then just summarize the outcomes of other jolts in the series and how other participants usually behave. This permits your participants to learn vicariously without frustrating themselves.

Divide a lengthy game into a series of jolts does have its risks, since the jolt may distract from the goals. Participants may also be eager to move on to the next logical phase of the activity without a debriefing discussion. You can avoid these issues by making sure that each jolt self-contained with a logical ending.

In spite of these limitations, when used appropriately, serial jolts are more effective than single jolts or lengthy activities.

Chapter 4
Conducting Jolts

Jolts are appropriate for use in a wide variety of training, learning, and coaching situations. Whether your work is with individual clients as a coach or with groups of participants as a training professional, the activities offered in this book are likely to fit your needs as presented or may be easily adapted for any other specialized situation or need. This chapter offers some tips on conducting and adapting jolts for these various uses, including your work with:

- Individuals
- Small Groups (two or more participants)
- Large Groups and Teams

The examples and notes we provide are just a few of the ways you can use and adapt jolts to increase the effectiveness of your work as a trainer or coach. As you work with jolts, you will likely discover new uses or variations on the ones in this book.

Individual Jolts

The majority of the jolts in this book specify in the instructions "one or more" as the required number of participants to effectively conduct a particular jolt. When you see this "one or more" label on a jolt, don't assume that the activity is somehow less effective or fun with only one participant. The labels we provide do accurately portray the appropriate number of participants. This labeling is also a cue for coaches looking for new ways to engage individual clients. Below are some examples of jolts we use as individual activities:

- Jolt 46, What's Funny?, is a thought experiment jolt that is perfectly suited for individual use. This activity simply requires you to look around and find all circular objects in the environment. When the individual or person you are coaching has completed and identified the circular objects inventory to your satisfaction, request a more personal reflection and connection to circular objects. Ask the person you are coaching to think about all the recent funny incidents he or she can recall that are related to circular objects.
- Jolt 21, Limits, requires physical activity and is appropriate for use with an individual.

- Jolt 11, Draw a Tree, uses drawing (don't worry, no artistic talent required) to drive the point of the jolt.

- Jolt 26, New Word, is an example of a puzzle jolt that you can use with individuals. This jolt asks the person to solve a puzzle in a very specific way that leads to success. Your debriefing points out that the technique used for solving one problem may not always work with another problem and illustrates the importance of thinking outside the box.

- Jolt 33, Psychic Cards, uses magic in an instructional way. You don't have to worry about your actual ability to perform a magic trick because we present a set of slides (that are provided on the website for this book, www.pfeiffer.com/go/jolts) that automatically performs the trick for you.

Not every situation is perfect, but the jolts in this book allow you to be creative in solving any shortcomings of the techniques. As noted earlier, a major shortcoming of conducting individual jolts is that the client cannot compare his or her answer to the answers or performance of other participants. We suggest that you compensate for this shortcoming by revealing how others responded to the same jolt in either individual or group situations.

Group Jolts as Individual Activities

Some jolts in this book require interaction between at least two participants. If you are working with an individual, you might use these techniques to conduct the jolt:

You Act as the Partner. Jolt 27, Newton, requires two participants to stand face to face, placing palm to palm. The point of the jolt is to get the partner's feet moving within seventeen seconds after you blow a whistle. The obvious solution if there is not another participant is for you to be your client's partner. Of course, you know the learning point so your job is to play the role of the naïve participant and let your client take the lead.

Get Someone Else to Act as Partner. If a jolt requires a second person, and if you want to capture authentic behavior, you can co-opt a colleague or available friend (if appropriate) to help you with the activity. Because most jolts last for such a short time, asking someone else for help really can live up to the common appeal for assistance, "Hey, you got a minute?" For example, Jolt 9, Double Your Money, requires two participants so that one of the partners can give the other partner an envelope and twenty $1 bills. If it is possible and appropriate to use a colleague and friend, this jolt can easily be conducted with an individual client. Even if you engage the help of someone else, your client might benefit from a few anecdotes about how others behaved in this situation. Bring this backup data and additional examples with you for use during the debriefing discussion.

Team Jolts as Individual Activities

Even some jolts intended for teams may be used with individual clients by employing a little creativity. For example, Jolt 5, Decode, works best if it is facilitated using six teams, each composed of four or more players. Because the point of this jolt is the importance of collaboration among teams, this requirement presents a major challenge if you are working with an individual.

One way to solve this problem is through use of the vicarious-learning-through-storytelling approach. Provide a few anecdotes (either real or fictional) about how other clients or groups have worked through the Decode experience. You should pause at a critical juncture in the narrative and ask the client, "What do think the participants did in this situation?" Listen to the response and, when appropriate, suggest a more effective alternative. During the debriefing, you might also ask the client to take on the role of another participant in your fictional or real jolt for greater depth of understanding.

Control Group Jolts as Individual Activities

With a bit of creativity you can even adopt jolts to a more complex form that relies on a control group to successfully demonstrate the point. Generally, we create these control group jolts using a two-person jolt or team-based jolt and instruct the different groups to perform different tasks. For example, in Jolt 20, Last Week, random groups of participants receive two different questionnaires for reviewing what happened during the previous week. In Jolt 47, What's Measured?, different groups of participants receive three different versions of a word puzzle.

SIDEBAR 1—MAGICAL MOMENTS

Inside every lengthy simulation game or other types of experiential activity, there is usually a brief—and magical—moment that produces major insights. If you can identify this moment, you can condense a major activity into a rapid jolt.

Whenever we design a lengthy activity, we challenge ourselves to shrink it to ninety-nine seconds or shorter. For example, Thiagi's cross-cultural simulation BARNGA lasts for thirty minutes to an hour. By focusing on the key element in this simulation, we were able to create a two-minute variation. We have done similar things with other experiential learning activities that other people have designed.

Here's another example: Most simulation games in the field of intercultural communication involve creating synthetic cultures with different (and frequently clashing) values, assigning participants to these cultures, and having them conduct elaborate negotiations under complex scenarios. Here's a quick jolt based on this type of simulation.

As each participant walks in, give her a small piece of paper with a single cultural value and an appropriate behavior associated with it. (Example: *You respect personal space. So stand at least an arm's length away from the others in your group when you are having a conversation.*) Use as many different value-behavior instructions as you can come up with; they don't have to be related to each other. When everyone has arrived, ask participants to organize themselves into groups of three to seven and decide what is the one most important goal they would like to achieve in the training session. Also tell participants to implement the cultural value (and the related behavior) that was specified in the pieces of paper they received. Announce a time limit and get out of the way.

After the activity, debrief participants to identify which behaviors they found to be bizarre, irritating, offensive, weird, or unpleasant. Let them discover that all these behaviors are based on some value that makes a lot of logical sense to people who believe those values.

Here is a suggestion for using the What's Measured? jolt with an individual client. First, give one version of the puzzle to the client and have her complete the task. Conduct a quick debriefing discussion. Present the other version of the puzzle and ask the client to identify the difference. Use follow-up questions to inquire how your client's behavior would have changed had she received the second version.

Conducting Jolts with Large Groups

Conducting a jolt with a large group has two advantages. For one thing, because of the contagious nature of experiential activities, large groups produce greater impact. In addition, during the debriefing discussion, large groups come up with more diverse insights.

SIDEBAR 2—HOW TO BENEFIT FROM A JOLT WITHOUT CONDUCTING IT

Here are some situations in which we don't use a jolt, even though they could be highly appropriate:

- We haven't earned enough trust among the participants to trap them with a jolt.
- The jolt deals with a controversial topic.
- The room setup does not permit participants moving around, pairing up, or working in teams.
- We don't have enough participants to produce maximum impact from the jolt.
- We have been using too many jolts already.
- We don't have enough time for an appropriate debriefing discussion.
- We are conducting a webinar.

In these situations, we manage to let the participants vicariously experience the jolt.

Instead of conducting the jolt, we tell them what happened with an actual or fictional group that experienced the jolt at an earlier time. We use our best storytelling techniques and describe the activity in detail. We pause at a critical juncture in the story and ask participants, "What do think the participants did in this situation?" (We never ask, "What would you have done in this situation?" to prevent entrapment.)

Participants' responses usually contain the same types of mindless decisions that occur when we actually conduct the jolt. When appropriate, we reveal a more effective alternative response the participants could have provided.

We debrief the group by asking them to speculate on how the fictional participants felt. We continue with additional debriefing questions by inviting participants to put themselves in the place of the previous group.

Using this storytelling approach, we let participants receive valuable insights from the vicarious jolt without having to embarrass themselves.

The critical factor in conducting a jolt is not how many people there are in the large group but, rather, how they interact with each other. For example, a jolt may involve hundreds of individuals solving a puzzle or answering a question. In this situation, the interaction is not among members of the group but between the individual participant and the puzzle. Other jolts may involve pairs of participants interacting with each other. So the unit of interaction is just two people rather than all two hundred in the room.

Some jolts may involve small groups or teams. The fastest way to organize teams is to let the participants organize themselves. A problem arises when the room is set up in auditorium style and you cannot move the chairs around. You can circumvent the problem by asking participants to stand up and interact with each other in small groups.

Here's another suggestion for effectively conducting jolts that involve small groups or teams. Have the members of each group select the "toughest-looking" person. Appoint this person to be the non-playing "game warden." The job of the game warden is to listen to your instructions and make sure that all the members of the group follow them faithfully.

As a last resort in conducting team-based jolts, invite a small group of volunteers to the front of the room and conduct the jolt with them. Other participants watch what is happening and learn vicariously.

Some jolts are deliberately designed for use with large groups. For example, you may tell everyone in the room to silently line up according to their dates of birth (months and days, not the years). After this jolt, you can debrief the participants to drive home principles related to complexity, self-organizing social systems, need for clear instructions, mob behavior, or the emergence of take-charge leaders.

Here are two more ideas for handling large groups:

- Use a whistle to attract participants' attention. Early in the session, set up a ground rule that everyone stops talking and listens to your instructions whenever they hear the whistle.

- If you are using handouts (as in the case of a printed puzzle), don't waste your time trying to distribute them during the activity. Place them on the seats before the session begins. If necessary, print these large-font instructions on the reverse side of the paper: *Do NOT look at the other side until the facilitator asks you to do so.*

Conclusion

Flexibility is the most important requirement for facilitating jolts. A *good* facilitator plays *within* the rules of the jolt. A *great* facilitator plays *with* the rules of the jolt. As you gain more experience in conducting jolts, feel free to experiment with variations that suit your participants—and your personal style.

Chapter 5
Facilitating Jolts

The use of a jolt requires that facilitators take special care to avoid misinterpretation or confusion among participants about their purpose or meaning. The narrative presented in Chapter 2 is a good example of an activity that to most of participants is a fun, engaging exercise, but potentially not so benign for at least one participant in the class.

This chapter presents some useful tips to keep in mind as you begin using jolts in your training programs. The first set of tips will help you make critical decisions about the use of jolts before, during, and after your training event. The second set of tips provides critical advice to anyone facilitating jolts.

Before the Jolt Tips

- **Be sure that you are using jolts for a legitimate reason.** Don't include jolts just because you wish to include an interesting activity.
- **Check your motivation.** Make sure that you are using jolts with a learning purpose in mind and not to embarrass participants or gain a power advantage. Ensure that you are focused on mindful learning.
- **Prepare for strong emotional reactions.** Prepare yourself to face potentially negative reactions from participants, especially when you use entrapment jolts.
- **Don't plan to use multiple jolts.** The impact of jolts wears off if you use too many in the same training session, so don't build a program with too many jolts. In fact, too many jolts may actually irritate your participants.
- **Plan adequate time for debriefing.** As you will see in Part 2 of the book, the real learning from jolts occurs during the debriefing. Remember that jolts by themselves are ineffective and possibly confusing without a thorough debriefing discussion.

During the Jolt Tips

- **Conduct the jolt at a rapid pace.** Speed is essential to the successful facilitation of a jolt, but make sure you are deliberate and clear as well as speedy.
- **Abandon the activity if you anticipate trouble.** Don't wait for current or brewing problems or difficulties to get out of hand. It is a good idea to abandon a jolt before you've completed it if you think you have made your point.

- **Try a vicarious approach.** If you are working with a new group and have not yet earned a sufficient level of trust from the participants, tell them a story about what happened when you used the jolt with a previous group. You can sometimes do this instead of conducting the jolt and obtain equally satisfactory results.

After the Jolt Tips

- **Allow time to defuse and decompress.** If the jolt has been particularly stressful due to participants' emotional reactions, make sure you allow enough time for everyone to defuse and decompress. Keep a professional distance from any personal attacks or comments. You may defuse any held-over hostility by apologizing for the entrapment and by explaining your rationale.

- **Change a tense atmosphere with follow-up activities.** In addition to conducting a debriefing discussion using a structured approach open to comments, you can help the participants get beyond a jolt by moving quickly into follow-up activities. One way of accomplishing this mood switch is by offering additional principles and conclusions based on the Jolt.

Practical Advice for Facilitators

In spite of their apparent simplicity, jolts can be tricky to facilitate. What follows are some tips, cautions, and caveats to keep in mind whenever you facilitate jolts.

We have run dozens of jolts over the past twenty years, and the tips we offer here are based on that mosaic of our experience. Clearly, issues of trust and emotions are part of the risk trainers take when they choose to use jolts. In addition, you need to be aware of potential problems posed by crossing boundaries of political and cultural correctness. Our advice to other facilitators who choose to use jolts is . . . to bring your sword and shield to the session, but be prepared to assume the mantle of a lawyer and the white flag of the peacemaker.

- **Earn participant trust before using jolts.** Most jolts incorporate an element of entrapment that involves the withholding of information to encourage participants to make incorrect assumptions. While most adults realize—at least at a surface level—that your deception had a learning point, it is easy to imagine why some feelings of betrayal are sure to surface. Be sure you have earned enough trust from the group before using a jolt.

- **Prepare for emotional reactions.** If you feel that facing strong emotional reactions is beyond your skills and your personal comfort level, think about conducting the session with a co-facilitator who has more experience with handling emotions.

- **Watch for possible landmines of political correctness.** Although you cannot completely shield yourself from being on the wrong side of political correctness, modeling and encouraging high levels of confidentiality and non-judgmental behavior is a good place to start. Another way to avoid these potential landmines is to establish a ground rule at the beginning of your session that what happens in your workshop stays there.

- **Explain the jolt's purpose.** It goes without saying that you need to make sure that the jolt you select is relevant to a specific training objective. Equally important is the need to clearly explain the connection between the jolt you have chosen and job-relevant behaviors during the debriefing discussion. Using irrelevant jolts for any other reason than a solid learning objective is an invitation for trouble and an abuse of the participants' trust.

- **Know when to abandon ship.** If a jolt seems to be producing more negative impact than positive, don't be afraid to stop the activity midway and move on. Remember, your purpose is to make a learning point, not to conduct a sociology experiment. Training folklore is replete with anecdotes about damage done to people who have participated in ethnic-discrimination simulations and prison-warden role plays.

- **Make sure all jolts include time for debriefing.** Set aside plenty of time for the discussion after the jolt because debriefing is just as important—if not more important than—conducting the jolt in the first place. Many trainers may be tempted to add jolts into a crowded training session and skip the debriefing discussion. This may be an inappropriate decision.

- **Be aware of the cultural context.** If you use jolts with international or intercultural participants (as we frequently do), do not minimize how participants from different cultures, ethnic backgrounds, and personal histories may react during the activity. If you think the jolt that you have chosen might potentially offend or embarrass participants, do some research or ask a knowledgeable friend, colleague, or expert before including the activity in your training.

Conclusion

In this chapter we have given you a brief overview of the potential pitfalls you might face as a facilitator who conducts jolts. The next chapter will cover the most important skill that a facilitator must master: conducting a debriefing discussion.

Chapter 6
Debriefing Jolts

Think of the debriefing techniques covered in this chapter as your baseline jolts debriefing toolkit. Offered here are methods that range from simple questioning techniques to more creative debriefing games. But more than anything else, the tools offered here support our belief that people learn more from reflecting on an experience than from the experience itself. In fact, we might argue that jolts and other experiential learning activities merely provide an excuse for reflection.

Your job as facilitator is to encourage reflective learning that connects jolts to experiences in the real world. Through this process of self-discovery and reflection, participants discover and share useful insights with each other.

As you gain more experience and confidence in using jolts, you will also learn how to maintain a balance between the structured nature of these activities and the need for participants to freely share their thoughts and feelings. You will also be able to recognize when the conversation with your participants is beginning to degenerate into stream-of-consciousness meandering and the advantages of using prepared questions to bring the group back on track.

Choosing the Right Debriefing Activity

While it is possible (and in most cases desirable) to conduct a debriefing discussion after a jolt, not all activities benefit equally from a debriefing session. From a facilitator's perspective, it all depends on the training objectives. For example, if your goal is to train a group of scientists on systematic research procedures, then a debriefing focusing on improving team relationships is an irrelevant choice. To help you with deciding whether to conduct a debriefing or not, we offer these four characteristics of activities that absolutely require you to conduct a debriefing discussion:

1. Any activity that uses metaphorical rather than direct references to the real world.
2. Any activity that generates intense feelings and emotions—either positive or negative. These activities can distract participants from focusing on logical patterns and root causes.
3. Any rapidly paced activity that moves so quickly that the significance of the critical events and learning points is lost on the participants.
4. Any activity that would lead participants to interpret the significance of an activity in different ways.

Bottom Line on Debriefing

The bottom line is that all jolts require some level of debriefing time because each one displays (to varying degree) all four characteristics noted above. At a minimum, if you fail to conduct a full debriefing after each jolt your participants will lose an opportunity to maximize their learning. A more serious consequence of leaving out the debriefing might be that your participants leave your training event in a confused state, perhaps wondering, "What was that all about?" And of course, failure to debrief participants after an emotionally difficult or challenging session leaves the door open for serious consequences.

Debriefing Methods, Tips, and Pointers

Presented below are suggested methods along with specific tips and pointers to help you quickly master conducting a debriefing discussion. We suggest that you use this section as a resource in the your planning and facilitation of jolts in Part 2. The pointers, tips, and activities include:

- Six Questions to Ask During Debriefing
- How Do You Feel? Processing Emotions
- Handling Emotions During Debriefing
- Replay—What Happened?
- Thinking Back—What Did You Learn?
- Workplace Connection—How Does the Jolt Relate?
- The "What If . . . ?" Exercise
- Action Planning—What Next?
- Using a "Dear Diary" Approach
- Using Debriefing Games
  - Sharing Insights Game
  - Brief Encounters Game
  - Speed Survey Game

Six Questions to Ask During Debriefing
Debriefing is the process of facilitating participants to reflect on their experience, gain valuable insights, and share them with each other. Below is a convenient set of questions for conducting a debriefing discussion. Note that while it is important for you to have an organized sequence of debriefing questions, it is equally important to encourage spontaneous comments from the participants. You need to cultivate an oxymoronic mindset of structure and flexibility at the same time. Encourage a freewheeling dialogue and fall back to the prepared structure when the conversation meanders in meaningless directions.

How Do You Feel? Processing Emotions
Most jolts result in some level of emotional consequences. You should process these emotions before you move on to more logical-based analysis of the jolt's results. Your

Question	Why?	How?
How do you feel?	This question invites participants to get in touch with their feelings about the jolt and its outcomes. By getting strong feelings and emotions off their chests, participants are in a better state of mind to be objective during the later phases of the debriefing discussion.	Begin this phase with a broad question about how they felt during and after the jolt. Encourage participants to use single words and phrases and discourage them from lengthy analyses. Follow up with specific questions related to different elements of the jolt.
What happened?	This question invites participants to recall and share information about what happened during the jolt. This prepares participants to analyze the information during the next stage.	Begin this phase with a broad question that asks participants to recall events during the jolt. Use this information to create a chronological list. Ask questions about specific events.
What did you learn?	This question encourages participants to list the different principles and insights they learned from participating in the jolt. This enables participants to share their insights with each other.	Begin this phase by asking participants an open question about what they learned. Make a list of principles and insights.
How does this relate?	This question encourages participants to relate their experiences during the jolt with events in the workplace. The responses enable participants to discuss the relevance of the jolt to real-world experiences.	Begin this phase with a broad question about the connection between the jolt and events in the workplace. Suggest that the jolt is a metaphor and ask the participants to offer real-world analogues.
What if . . . ?	This question encourages participants to apply their insights to new contexts. It presents different scenarios and requires participants to speculate on how people's behaviors would change under different contexts.	Begin this phase with several scenarios that require speculation on how the differences would have affected the process and the outcomes of the jolt. Then invite participants to offer their own scenarios and discuss them.
What next?	This question encourages participants to undertake action planning. It encourages them to apply their insights from the jolt to the real world.	Begin this phase by asking the participants to suggest strategies for use in future jolts. Then ask the participants how they would change their workplace behaviors as a result of the insights they gained from the jolt.

initial set of questions should give the participants an opportunity to express their emotions and clear the air for a more centered and objective discussion later in the debriefing phase.

Here are some guidelines for improving the effectiveness of this phase of debriefing:

Allow Time for Emotional Reactions.   Debriefing is particularly important with jolts that reflect painful real-world events such as accidents, downsizing, mergers, and betrayal. When the jolt produces intense emotions—whether positive or negative—participants tend to make mindless assumptions and acquire superstitious behavior patterns. Used appropriately, emotional debriefing can support insightful learning by preparing participants to logically analyze their feelings.

Begin with a Broad Question.   Invite participants to get in touch with their feelings and emotions about the process and the outcomes of the jolt.

Use Appropriate Terminology.   Some groups (engineers and auditors, for example) feel uncomfortable with touchy-feely words. Instead of asking, "How do you *feel*?" change the question to "How do you think most engineers would react to this activity?"

Explore Specific Classes of Feelings.   Use a list of words and phrases related to potential feelings that may arise from the activity. (Select suitable words from the list on the next page.) Ask participants whether they experienced these feelings during their participation in the jolt.

Provide Anonymity.   Prepare a checklist of suitable words from the sidebar. Distribute a copy to each participant and ask him or her to circle five words that reflect the most probable feelings related to the jolt. Collect these handouts, mix them up, and read the circled words, one at a time. Ask participants to recall and discuss events from the jolt related to this specific feeling.

Discuss Feelings Related to Specific Events.   Use a recorded list of events from the jolt to recall major decision points and milestones in the activity. Encourage participants to discuss how they felt during these specific events. (See Conduct Live Likert.)

CONDUCT LIVE LIKERT

Place five index cards with the numerals 1 through 5 on the floor, equal distances apart. Call out an appropriate feeling (for example, *anger*) and ask the participants to stand next to the index card with the number that best describes the intensity of their feeling on a 5-point scale. (For example, 5 = extremely angry, 1 = not angry at all.) Discuss the range of intensity of this feeling among participants. Repeat the procedure with other feelings.

SIDEBAR 1—FEELINGS AND EMOTIONS LIST

adventurous	detached	intimidated
afraid	determined	lost
aggressive	different	miserable
agitated	disappointed	nervous
alert	discouraged	optimistic
alone	disillusioned	playful
amazed	disinterested	powerless
ambivalent	distracted	pressured
amused	dominated	puzzled
angry	eager	rejected
annoyed	effective	reluctant
anxious	embarrassed	sad
ashamed	encouraged	scared
betrayed	energetic	secure
bored	engaged	self-conscious
calm	enthusiastic	skeptical
challenged	excited	stubborn
cheated	flustered	surprised
comfortable	foolish	tense
competitive	frustrated	tentative
confident	grateful	thankful
confrontational	greedy	threatened
confused	guilty	thrilled
cooperative	happy	touched
curious	hopeless	touchy
defeated	ignored	trapped
defensive	impatient	uncomfortable
delighted	insecure	upset
depressed	inspired	wary
desperate	insulted	

Handling Emotions During Debriefing

Jolts frequently produce emotional responses from participants, especially if you use the activities to explore controversial subjects. At the conclusion of a jolt (and sometimes in the middle of a jolt), participants may confront you with hostility, frustration, futility, or grief. Take care to not permit a few vociferous participants to hijack the debriefing discussion and overshadow the positive benefits of these reactions from participants.

In this book, we have avoided controversial jolts that are likely to provoke excessive emotions. We have also provided appropriate cautionary recommendations about what could go wrong. We suggest the technique of converting potentially hazardous jolts into storytelling sessions so that participants can vicariously benefit from a narrative rather than directly encountering painful experiences.

Here are some guidelines for achieving a balancing act between excessive emotions and bland intellectual analyses:

- **Keep your own emotions in check.** Your own feelings and emotions complicate any situation or confrontation in your class, so keep emotions in check.

- **Remember that your job is not to provide therapy.** You are merely facilitating participants' expression of emotions—both positive and negative—so that they can gain useful insights and awareness. A simple focus on this goal will relieve you of unnecessary anxiety.

- **Explain that participation is a choice.** Explain to your participants that no one is required to experience anything or to express anything unless he or she wants to. As the facilitator, it is your task to protect the privacy of people by discouraging peer pressure.

- **Listen and participate appropriately.** When participants begin expressing feelings and emotions related to the jolt, your main job is to model appropriate listening behaviors. Look directly at the speaker. Listen to both the content and the feeling of what is being said. Behave in a manner that is consistent with the expressed emotion. For the most part, use nonverbal signals to encourage a participant to keep talking. However, if the participant begins to analyze his own feelings or those of other participants, intervene politely. Remind everyone that logical analyses will come later in the debriefing discussion after all have had an opportunity to vent.

- **Keep perspective, even when attacked.** When participants verbally attack each other, try to stop the assault but permit the speaker to continue appropriately if possible. Insist that the speaker keep statements focused on the point of the activity and not other participants. Acknowledge that you have heard the angry participant's message without anger or sarcasm and thank the participant for sharing his or her feelings with everyone. Move on to the next person or to the next activity. If you don't feel comfortable in this confrontational role, try conducting the jolt with a co-facilitator. You and the co-facilitator can take turns processing emotional reactions from agitated participants.

- **Debrief yourself.** After conducting a jolt, debrief yourself to discover useful information about your own personality and lessons for your own growth as a facilitator and as a person.

Replay—What Happened?

During debriefing, this question helps you collect information from different participants about what happened during the jolt. This replay activity makes it possible for the participants to compare and contrast their perceptions and lessons learned in order to derive general principles related to the training topic.

Here are a few guidelines for improving the effectiveness of "What Happened?" questions:

- **Watch out for false memory.** Do not assume that everyone will recall exactly the same events in the same order. During debriefing, point out differences among different people's recollections and discuss why these discrepancies happen and what to do about them.

- **Begin with a broad question.** Ask participants to recall major events during the jolt. Record a chronological list on a flip chart.

- **Ask questions about specific events.** Identify each major event you recorded during the jolt and ask participants to recall significant points they remember about that event.

- **Use instant replay.** Use any readily available video recording device from a point-and-shoot camera to an inexpensive video camera to record the events during the jolt. Ask participants to recall particular segments of the jolt. Replay the video and discuss discrepancies that emerge.

Thinking Back—What Did You Learn?

Encourage participants to think back on their experiences with the jolt and make a list of insights they gained or principles they learned. This allows participants to discover learning points and to apply them back on the job.

Here are some suggestions for increasing the effectiveness of thinking back and learning from the jolt:

- **Develop a list of insights or principles learned.** Analyze current and past jolt activities and make a list of important learning points and principles. Make sure you update this list for use in future jolts.

- **Begin with a broad question.** Invite participants to come up with useful principles and insights from their experiences during the jolt.

- **Encourage discussion of each principle.** Ask the participants to treat each principle as a hypothesis and offer evidence from the jolt (and from relevant workplace experience) to support it or to reject it.

- **Use your principle list to keep the conversation going.** If the conversation among participants slows down, offer a principle that was not discussed previously. You might ask the participants to present relevant information from the jolt and from their real-world experiences.

Workplace Connection—How Does the Jolt Relate?

Encourage participants to relate what happened in the jolt to events in their workplace. Here are some suggestions for increasing the effectiveness of this debriefing exchange:

- **Begin with a broad question.** Ask the participants to explain how the jolt reflects events in their workplace. Suggest that the jolt is a metaphor and ask participants to speculate on what real-world events it is a metaphor for.

- **Discuss specific events from the jolt.** Identify specific events from the jolt and ask the participants to come up with similar experiences in their workplace. Encourage them to discuss similarities and differences between these two sets of events.

- **Discuss objects and artifacts.** Identify specific materials used in the jolt (such as playing cards or ropes) and ask the participants to find their workplace counterparts.

- **Discuss specific tasks and roles.** Ask the participants to relate different tasks and roles in the jolt to similar elements in their workplace. Encourage a discussion of the similarity of people's behaviors in the jolt and the workplace context.

- **Discuss specific principles.** Ask participants to recall different principles that are reflected in the jolt. Encourage them to compare and contrast how these principles work in the real-work situations.

The "What If . . . ?" Exercise

Use a "What if . . . ?" scenario to explore ways that participants can apply their new insights in to different workplace situations. Present alternative scenarios and ask the participants to extrapolate from the brief jolt to different workplace situations.

Here are some suggestions for using "What if…?" scenarios:

- **Come prepared with a variety of relevant scenarios.** Before running the jolt, create different jolt scenarios by changing time requirements, number of participants, degree of interaction, type of task, difficulty level, supply and materials requirements, major learning points, debriefing questions, scoring system, or the rewards for winners.

- **Encourage freewheeling speculation around each scenario.** Don't limit the speculation by participants as they change scenarios. Make sure you provide sufficient time for in-depth discussions and dialogue.

- **Invite additional workplace scenarios.** Encourage participants to identify relevant variables in their own workplace and speculate how the changes might impact their behavior and/or expected outcomes.

Action Planning—What Next?

Action planning questions encourage the participants to come up with improved strategies for future use.

Here are some suggestions you can use during your debriefing:

- **Ask participants how they would approach a second round of the jolt.** Ask participants how they would change their strategies if they were to participate once more in the same jolt. Encourage them to make use of everything they learned from their initial exposure to the jolt.

- **Ask participants to give advice to newcomers.** Invite participants to imagine the advice they would give others who were participating in the jolt for the first time.

- **Encourage real-world connections.** Ask participants how their workplace behaviors might change as a result of the insights gained from their participation in the jolt.

- **Discuss workplace application of specific principles.** Invite participants to recall the principles reflected in the jolt. Ask them to discuss how they would apply each principle to their workplace situations.

Using a "Dear Diary" Approach

Since debriefs are all about reflection, you can easily incorporate a journal writing exercise into your debriefing. A journal approach has the following advantages:

- It permits participants to reflect on their personal reactions without being distracted by argumentative, defensive, or self-glorifying conversations.
- It is better suited for introverted individuals who don't want to disclose their feelings
- It is more compatible with the norms of reticent cultures that frown upon self-disclosure.
- It protects the confidentiality of participants' thoughts and opinions.
- It better fits each participant's personal pace and schedule.

Ask participants to write a personal journal entry reflecting on their behaviors, reactions, and insights related to the jolt. Emphasize that this personal journal is not for sharing with others. Set aside some time immediately after the jolt for this written exercise or allow time for journaling after the workshop. If you need to work with the group directly during the workshop, you might try structuring the journal-writing activity by distributing a list of concepts to participants after the jolt. For example, if you conduct Jolt 5, Decode, suggest that the participants' entries contain the words and phrases: *teamwork, assumptions about teams, collaboration within a team, collaboration between teams, competition within a team, competition between teams, win-win and win-lose thinking, and team and organizational focus.*

Another approach to structuring a written debriefing is to distribute a questionnaire to participants. Here is a sample questionnaire based on our six-step model for debriefing:

1. How do you feel about the jolt? What is your reaction to the process and its final outcome?
2. What important things happened during the jolt?
3. What did you learn from the jolt? What insights did you gain about other people's behavior? What about your own behavior?
4. How does the jolt relate to real-world events?
5. In what different ways could you modify this jolt? What would happen as a result of these changes?
6. If we were to conduct this jolt again, how would you behave differently?
7. As a result of your new insights from the jolt, how would you behave differently in your workplace?

You can also ask participants to review their journal entries for a particular jolt activity after the passage of time and to jot down a current thought or insight. Here are some suggested questions for this exercise:

1. How do you feel about the jolt after the passage of about a month? What is your reaction to earlier reactions? Is there a major change in your reaction? If so, what caused the change?
2. How did your earlier insights from the jolt influence your behavior during the past month?

3. What additional relationships did you discover between the jolt and real-world events?
4. If you were to participate in the same jolt again, how would you behave differently?
5. What recommendations do you have for improving the effectiveness of the jolt?

Here is how we preserve participants' anonymity while still allowing the free flow of ideas, insights, and revelation gained during jolts. First, we invite the participants to drop anonymous photocopies of their journal entries in a collection box. Then we edit out identifying information before we distribute copies to all participants.

Finally, you may wish to keep your own journal after conducting your next jolt and then experiment with other written approaches to debriefing activities.

Using Debriefing Games

Sometimes discussion after a jolt activity lags and engagement diminishes due to the contrast between a fast-paced jolt and deliberate work of discussion and reflection.

One approach for maintaining the level of engagement and a fast pace during debriefing is to convert the discussion into a structured activity. Roger Greenaway calls such an activity "the game after the game."

What follows are some debriefing game suggestions. These games work best if you have twenty or more participants because their success relies on contagious enthusiasm and multiple perceptions about the game from the participants.

SHARING INSIGHTS GAME

Here is a debriefing game that requires participants to pair up with different people to share insights.

Participants

- 10 or more
- 20 or more participants produce the best results

Time

- 10 to 15 minutes

Flow

Ask a question. Ask a question that requires reflecting on the jolt and coming up with useful insights. Here are three sample questions:

- What did you learn from the jolt?
- How do the activities in the jolt relate to events in your workplace?
- How would apply the insights from the jolt to improving your workplace performance?

Jolts! Activities to Wake Up and Engage Your Participants

Pause for coming up with a response. Ask participants to reflect on your question and relate it to the jolt they experienced earlier. Ask them to come up with several responses and select the best one. Encourage participants to jot down some notes that identify the key points in the response.

Share your response with a partner. Ask each participant to pair up with another participant from some other area of the room. Ask the two participants in each pair to take turns sharing their responses to the question. Encourage participants to take notes on the other person's response as they will share it with a different partner during the next round. When this exchange is completed, ask the pair to look for new partners.

Share new responses with new partners. Ask participants to pair up with new partners and share the responses they heard from their previous partners. Ask everyone to repeat the process of finding new partners, present the most recent response they heard, and listen to a response from the other participant.

Select the top three responses. After a suitable period of time (when most participants have worked with at least five different partners), announce the end of the exchange activity. Ask each participant to work independently, think back on different responses, and select the three best ones. The selected responses may or may not include the participant's original response.

BRIEF ENCOUNTERS GAME

Here is a debriefing game that involves repeated pairing and sharing. It is based on a Leif Hansen game we use often.

Participants

- 10 or more
- 20 or more participants produce the best results

Time

- 10 to 15 minutes

Flow

Organize pairs of participants. Ask each participant to find a partner and ask each pair to stand back-to-back.

Ask a question. Ask the following question:

- What was the most predominant feeling during—and after—the jolt?

Ask participants to share their responses. As soon as you have asked the question, tell participants to turn around, face each other, and take turns sharing their responses with their partners. Encourage participants to share more than one response to the question.

Switch partners. When both participants have shared, ask them to find new partners. Ask the members of each pair to stand back-to-back.

Repeat the process. Ask these questions related to the jolt, one question at a time:

- What is an important thing that happened during the jolt?
- What is one thing that you learned from this jolt?
- How does this jolt relate to events in your workplace?
- Based on what you learned from the jolt, how would you change your behavior in the workplace?

Ask participants to share their responses with their partners as before. After sharing each set of responses, ask participants to find new partners before you ask the next question.

SPEED SURVEY GAME

Here is a fast-paced debriefing activity that keeps all participants busy interviewing each other:

Participants

- 10 or more
- 20 or more participants produce the best results.

Time

- 10 to 15 minutes

Preparation

Prepare question cards, each with one of these debriefing questions:

- What was the most predominant feeling during—and after—the jolt?
- What is an important thing that happened during the jolt?
- What is one thing that you learned from this jolt?
- How does this jolt relate to events in your workplace?
- Based on what you learned from the jolt, how would you change your behavior in the workplace?

Have an equal number of cards with each of these six questions.

Flow

Brief the participants. Explain that during this activity, participants will mingle and poll the others for their reactions to the jolt.

Explain the activity. Each participant receives one of six different questions about the jolt. Instruct participants to interview everyone—including participants who have the same question—and to collect the responses.

Distribute the question cards. Shuffle the packet of question cards and ask each participant to take a card. Ask participants to study the questions on their cards and think of suitable answers.

Coordinate the response-collection activity. Announce that everyone now has three minutes to collect responses from other people in the room on the question assigned. Encourage participants to interview as many others as possible, including people with the same question. Start the timer.

Coordinate the analysis activity. After three minutes, conclude the information-collection activity. Ask participants to find others with the same question and form a team. Invite team members to share and organize all the responses they collected. Distribute sheets of flip-chart paper and ask teams to summarize the information on these sheets.

Coordinate the reporting activity. Randomly select a team and ask the members to display their flip-chart poster. Ask a representative from this team to present the results and conclusions. Repeat this procedure with each team's report.

PART 2
A Collection of Jolts

Introduction to Part 2

The fifty jolts in this section offer trainers and facilitators an extraordinary opportunity to connect with and engage their audiences. The activities presented here are appropriate for use in many types of training, from communications training to teamwork and time management (see Table 1 for a complete listing of topic areas, with appropriate jolts for specific topic areas).

As noted in Part 1, jolts are extremely flexible and allow you to be creative both in how the activities are delivered and in their use in the training session. For example, a jolt that is typically administered in a group setting may be transformed into an individual coaching activity. However, as a convenient starting point for new users, Table 2 categorizes the fifty jolts by minimum and maximum number of participants and lists the supplies needed to run the activity.

Organization of the Jolts

Each jolt is arranged in exactly the same way for ease of facilitation. In addition to a brief opening statement about the purpose of the jolt, all the activities include the following subheadings and information:

Synopsis—a short introductory paragraph that provides an overview of the activity and a few top-line facilitation tips for the trainer.

Purpose—a concise statement that highlights the overall learning points of the activity.

Training Topics—suggested topic areas appropriate for this activity (such as teamwork, communication, or cooperation).

Participants—suggested number of participants to successfully conduct an activity, along with variations.

Time—suggested time to allow for conducting the activity as well as a suggested debriefing time.

Supplies—special supplies needed to conduct the activity (such as a set of standard playing cards or index cards).

Equipment—devices needed to conduct the activity (such as timer or whistle).

Flow—step-by-step instructions on how to facilitate the jolt.

Debriefing—key questions to ask during your debriefing.

Learning Points—a listing of key principles or concepts that can be elicited from the activity.

Variations—alternate ways to conduct the activity.

Field Notes—important additional information or caveats about a particular jolt.

Table 1 lists suggested training topics that are appropriate for each jolt. You can adapt and change the activities to fit other topics, but you may find this listing a good place to start.

Table 1 Index of Training Topics

(Continued)

Table 1 (Continued)

Learning Point	Page Number
Stereotyping	
Jolt 2. By the Numbers	53
Jolt 10. Draw a Hand	89
Jolt 48. Wobegon	239
Teamwork	
Jolt 1. Alliances	49
Jolt 5. Decode	67
Jolt 23. Me and My Team	137
Jolt 41. Team Planning	205
Jolt 42. Team Power	213
Jolt 43. Teamwork	219
Jolt 49. Workers and Watchers	243
Time Management	
Jolt 21. Limits	131
Jolt 28. Next Action	155
Trust	
Jolt 9. Double Your Money	85
Jolt 23. Me and My Team	137
Writing	
Jolt 4. Dear John	61
Jolt 35. Scrambled Words	179
Jolt 36. Sequencing	183

Table 2 is a handy reference guide that will help you pick the appropriate jolt for your group size, time requirement, and available supplies. This is just a general guide for planning purposes. Jolts can easily be adjusted to fit just about any training, learning, or coaching situation.

Table 2   Quick Reference

Jolt	Page	Minimum Number of Participants	Minimum Time Required	Supplies
Jolt 1. Alliances	49	3	12	Playing cards
Jolt 2. By the Numbers	53	1	5	None
Jolt 3. Clock on the Ceiling	57	1	8	None
Jolt 4. Dear John	61	1	8	Handouts
Jolt 5. Decode	67	8	15	Handouts
Jolt 6. Dollar Auction	73	2	10	A dollar bill
Jolt 7. Don't Lift the Pen	77	1	8	Paper and pencils
Jolt 8. Double Talk	83	2	9	None
Jolt 9. Double Your Money	85	2	13	$40, envelopes
Jolt 10. Draw a Hand	89	1	5	Index cards and pencils
Jolt 11. Draw a Tree	91	1	7	Index cards and pencils

(Continued)

Table 2 (Continued)

Jolt	Page	Minimum Number of Participants	Minimum Time Required	Supplies
Jolt 12. Ears for Smiley	93	2	13	Paper, pencils, whistle
Jolt 13. Enjoy and Learn	97	1	5	None
Jolt 14. Excited	99	15	8	Prepared cards
Jolt 15. First Touch	103	3	8	Handout
Jolt 16. Free!	107	1	7	Two gift cards, handout
Jolt 17. Free Time	111	4	8	Slides, dots, whistle, timer
Jolt 18. How Fast?	115	2	10	Handouts, pencils, timer, whistle
Jolt 19. How Many Squares?	121	1	5	Slides
Jolt 20. Last Week	125	1	8	Handouts
Jolt 21. Limits	131	1	5	None
Jolt 22. Long Words	133	2	10	Handout, pencils, whistle
Jolt 23. Me and My Team	137	8	10	Index cards, pens, timer, whistle
Jolt 24. Memory Test	141	1	10	Paper and pens, timer, audio recording
Jolt 25. Mingle	145	5	8	Prepared etiquette cards
Jolt 26. New Word	149	1	8	Slides
Jolt 27. Newton	153	2	7	Timer, whistle
Jolt 28. Next Action	155	1	5	Paper and pencils
Jolt 29. Palm to Palm	157	1	5	Audio recording
Jolt 30. Paper Money	159	2	6	One dollar bills
Jolt 31. Photo Analysis	163	2	10	Slide, handouts
Jolt 32. Positive Spin	169	1	4	None
Jolt 33. Psychic Cards	171	1	8	Slides
Jolt 34. Say It in Sequence	175	1	13	None
Jolt 35. Scrambled Words	179	1	5	Handout
Jolt 36. Sequencing	183	2	8	Handouts, paper, pens, timer, whistle
Jolt 37. Shapes and Colors	189	2	7	Prepared cutouts, bag
Jolt 38. Six Tiles	193	1	17	Slides
Jolt 39. Stroop	199	1	6	Slides
Jolt 40. Synchronized Clapping	203	10	5	None
Jolt 41. Team Planning	205	6	8	Handout, timer, whistle
Jolt 42. Team Power	213	6	8	Handouts, timer, whistle
Jolt 43. Teamwork	219	6	8	Handout, timer, whistle
Jolt 44. The Training Story	223	1	8	Audio recording
Jolt 45. Visualize a Tree	227	1	6	None
Jolt 46. What's Funny?	229	1	10	None
Jolt 47. What's Measured?	233	3	6	Handouts, timer, whistle
Jolt 48. Wobegon	239	5	8	Paper and pencils
Jolt 49. Workers and Watchers	243	4	6	Blindfolds, rope, timer, whistle
Jolt 50. Your Choice	247	1	13	Pens and pencils, pencil cups

Jolt 1
Alliances

The realities of the global workplace often require temporary alliances among different individuals and even different organizations. This serial jolt (which is played in two rounds) explores the nature of negotiation and coalition formation.

Synopsis

Participants are asked to form asset coalitions with other participants under a strict time limit. The numbers displayed on a standard deck of playing cards (2, 3, 4, 5 . . .) provide the initial asset base of each participant; the facilitator randomly distributes the cards at the start of the activity. Participants who successfully form a coalition team with total assets that exceed a predetermined amount are allowed to divide the profits.

Purpose

- To explore the formation and dynamics of temporary alliances

Training Topics

- Teamwork
- Cooperation

Participants

- Three or more, but the ideal size is a group of five
- You may divide larger groups of participants into play groups of three to six

Time

- 5 minutes for the activity
- 7 to 15 minutes for debriefing

Supplies

- A set of five playing cards (Ace, 2, 3, 4, and 5 of any suit) for each group (Ace counts as the number "1")

Equipment

- Countdown timer
- Whistle

Flow

Brief the participants. Shuffle the packet of cards face down and give a card to each participant. Ask the participants to show the cards to each other. Explain that each participant is the CEO of a major corporation and that the number on the card represents the total assets of the corporation he or she now leads.

Announce the request for a bid. Explain that each participant must form a coalition with the other CEO participants to create coalitions with a total asset worth of at least 8. Note that forming this coalition is necessary in order to bid on a profitable major multinational project and that if this coalition building with the other CEOs is successful, the project will yield a guaranteed profit of $16 million.

Emphasize two requirements. Note that the total coalition assets to win the bid must exceed 8 (as represented by the total point values of the playing cards). Let the participants know as well that the corporations forming the coalition must agree on how to divide the $16 million profit among the coalition members.

Encourage negotiations. Since there are different ways of forming a coalition that meet or exceed the required asset total of 8, encourage players to negotiate with one another to maximize their personal share of the profit.

Conduct the activity. Announce a time limit of 3 minutes and set the timer. Begin the activity. If a group of participants reports to you that they have completed the activity, make sure that the group has total assets of 8 and a formula for dividing the $16 million profit. Ask the participants who have completed the activity to write down their share of the $16 million on a piece of paper. Blow your whistle at the end of 3 minutes to conclude the negotiation period.

Conduct the second round. Collect and shuffle the playing cards used in the first round and redistribute the cards to the participants. Explain that global economic conditions have changed and that the profit potential is greater. Explain that the profits guarantee is now $20 million. Give participants a 2-minute time limit for forming new alliances. Play the game as before and conclude it after 2 minutes.

Debriefing

Conduct a debriefing discussion with questions such as the following:

- *How did it feel to be a member of a successful coalition? How did it feel to not be included in a successful coalition?*
- *What were the behavior similarities and differences during the two rounds?*
- *Did the first round behaviors affect behaviors during the second round?*
- *How did the members of the alliance divide the profit?*

- *Did your reputation from the first round impact how others behaved toward you during the second round?*
- *How does this game reflect events that have occurred in your workplace?*
- *What might have happened if every corporation formed had the same assets?*
- *What might have happened if we played one more round?*

 Learning Points

1. What happened between the participants in the first round had a direct impact on what happened in the subsequent rounds of the activity.
2. Those participants who were in some way excluded during the first round of the play will likely try to exclude others in the second round.
3. Business goals and relationship goals frequently clash with each other.

 Variation

What if you don't have playing cards? If playing cards are not available, then use small, card-sized pieces of paper and write the numbers 1 through 5 in the available space.

Jolt 2
By the Numbers

The need to be correct appears to be a universal human need and this foible of human nature is incorporated in this jolt. We use this jolt frequently in our training sessions on diversity and inclusion. It makes participants aware of the insidious nature of stereotyping and prejudice. A unique feature of this jolt is the debriefing discussion inserted in the middle of the activity.

 ## Synopsis

Participants are presented with sets of numbers and asked to find the sequencing or order patterns in the number sets. The facilitator asks the participants to suggest their own number sets that follow the same sequencing order and pattern. The learning turns on the participants' suggesting number sets based on wrong assumptions and faulty reasoning.

 ## Purpose

- To explore the limitations of inductive thinking

 ## Training Topics

- Critical thinking
- Stereotyping

 ## Participants

- Minimum of 1
- Maximum: no limit

 ## Time

- 5 to 15 minutes for both the activity and debriefing session

Supplies

- No special supplies or equipment is needed. However, a flip chart may be handy to write down the sets of numbers called out by the participants

 Caution

Note that an element of entrapment is inherent in your choice of the initial number sets. You might be accused of setting the class up to fail or to look stupid. Don't get defensive. Just acknowledge the complaint and explain that the purpose of the deception was to highlight the learning point. We suggest that you go easy on the "nagging" part of the activity (below) if participants appear to be truly upset.

 Flow

Brief the players. Tell the participants that you will present sets of three numbers and emphasize the importance of listening carefully to your instructions. Point out that the participants' job is to find the recurring pattern among the three numbers in each set. Present these four sample number sets:

Set A	3—6—7
Set B	14—28—29
Set C	5—10—11
Set D	2—4—5

Invite participation. Most players will solve the problem immediately and grin knowingly. Other participants may shout out their solutions to the number challenge. Without providing the correct answer, repeat the instructions and ask everyone to listen carefully. Challenge the participants to supply new number sets with a similar pattern as those you've displayed and say that you will accept or reject each suggestion made with a simple "yes" or "no."

Provide feedback. Our experience is that players will give you additional number sets they are absolutely confident are correct; A participant might offer the number (4), then double it (8), and then finish with the number (9), which is one more than the second number. Actually, the pattern you established in the example is any three numbers in ascending order (for example, 5, 6, 7). Listen to each set suggestion provided by the participants and provide a simple answer of "Yes" or "No."

Nag the players. After verifying and accepting a few suggested number sets, ask the players how they feel. Comment on the smug look on most faces. Here is some suggested dialogue that you can put in your own words:

Many of you are falling into the trap of confirmation bias. You think you have figured out the pattern that links the number sets. You immediately started proving your hypothesis by offering number sets that fit the pattern you thought was correct. You felt happy whenever your number set got a "Yes" and so offered more number sets of the same type and enjoyed a feeling of being smart and superior. You were very careful not to present any number set that might get a "No" so that no one would consider you stupid.

A true scientist, however, keeps an open mind and is not so self-assured and works to disprove an initial hypothesis. If you were following this methodology, you would have offered me some number sets that you "know" to be incorrect.

Give feedback. Challenge the participants to provide new number sets and answer "Yes" or "No" according to whether or not the sets offered contain three whole numbers in ascending order. According to this requirement, these test sets would obviously receive a "Yes":

7—9—14
10—20—2,000
8—6 million—7 billion

And these test sets would receive a "No" response:

5—9—8
9—8—2001
98—15—3

Return to your nagging. Continue the activity and when a participant follows your advice on the scientific methods and receives a "No," ask how it feels to hear the answer "No." Explain that most people feel depressed if their hypothesis or answer is rejected. Point out again that "No" provides valuable information and that sometimes "No" is more valuable than "Yes." Invite everyone to celebrate every "No" answer received during the activity.

Speed up the process. Explain that you are going to try out additional number sets by yourself. Use confusing sets of numbers (such as 5—78—2,365,897) and give a resounding "Yes" to each.

Explain the pattern. End the activity by inviting the players to guess the pattern you were using for the your own test numbers and then reveal the pattern you used which is—*any three whole numbers in ascending sequence*.

Debriefing

Relate the experience to the human tendency toward accepting hasty generalizations and preconceived assumptions. Explain that this simple activity illustrates how we often strengthen our unjustified conclusions by applying the same rubric to every new situation and deliberately ignore information that does not fit our preconceived notions.

Learning Points

1. What we see or perceive is what we believe.
2. The human brain tends to form stereotypes.
3. We have a bias toward confirming what we know rather than rejecting what we know.
4. Without the ability to reject or modify our existing beliefs, valuable information is likely to be lost.

Variation

Numbers make your participants anxious? With some imagination, you can replace sets of three numbers with sets of other objects: For example, you can use sets of three Oscar-winning actors as your sample set with the secret category defined as any three famous people.

Jolt 3
Clock on the Ceiling

In many ways, this is an ideal jolt. It takes very little time, requires no props, gets the participants out of their chairs, delivers a powerful punch, and provides a metaphor for a variety of principles from different professional disciplines. What more can you ask for?

 ## Synopsis

This jolt requires participants to point to an imaginary clock on the ceiling and rotate their index fingers in a clockwise direction. When asked to lower their outstretched fingers below shoulder level (while still pointing to the imaginary clock on the ceiling) the participants learn a lesson in perspective when they discover that it appears their fingers inevitably rotate in a counterclockwise direction.

 ## Purpose

- To explore how point of view determines what you see

 ## Training Topics

- Leadership
- Customer service
- Diversity
- Communication

 ## Participants

- One or more
- Even large numbers of people can simultaneously participate in this individual activity

 ## Time

- 3 minutes for the activity.
- 5 to 15 minutes for debriefing

Flow

Ask participants to stand up. When the participants stand, ask them to extend their right arms and point their index fingers up toward an imaginary clock on the ceiling. Then ask the participants to lower their right hands below shoulder level by bending their elbows while still pointing their fingers to the clock on the ceiling.

   Rotate the fingers around the clock. Next, ask the participants to raise their hands above their heads again and point to the 12 o'clock position on the imaginary clock. Then ask the participants to use their fingers to circle around the clock to the 3 o'clock position, then around to the 6 o'clock position, then up to the 9 o'clock position, then back to the 12 o'clock position. When the task is complete, ask the participants to continue moving their fingers in a clockwise rotation without stopping.

   Ask participants to lower their hands. While the participants continue to circle the imaginary clock in a clockwise direction with their right index fingers, instruct them to keep their fingers pointed toward the ceiling and their eyes on their extended fingers as they circle around the clock. Instruct participants to slowly lower their hands so their index fingers (still rotating) come to a position below shoulder level.

   Point to the direction of the rotation. Ask the following question about the rotation direction: *"What direction is your finger moving now, clockwise or counterclockwise?"* All the participants should be looking down at their rotating fingers (in contrast to looking up at their rotating fingers earlier). All the participants should clearly see a change in the direction of rotation. You can act surprised when participants report a counterclockwise rotation of their fingers.

   Repeat the activity. Ask participants to raise their right hands above their heads and rotate their index fingers in a clockwise direction, then tell them to lower their hands (still pointing to the ceiling and rotating as they did before) to see if the phenomenon happens again.

Debriefing

A change of perspective. Ask participants why they think the change in direction of rotation occurred. Steer the discussion toward this conclusion:

> *The participants' fingers actually continued rotating in the same direction (clockwise) after their hands were lowered. What changed was the point of view.*

Explain that when participants looked at their rotating fingers as they pointed toward the imaginary clock on the ceiling, the perspective was from the bottom up. Once the hands and rotating fingers were lowered below shoulder level, the point of view was from the top down. This change in perspective explains the perceived change in their finger rotation direction.

   How does this relate? Continue the debriefing discussion by asking participants to identify situations in which a change of perspective results in a radical change in perception.

Learning Points

1. Our perceptions depend on our point of view.
2. By taking time to appreciate the power of perspective and its impact on perception, radically different understanding is possible.

Variation

Want to speed up the activity? Stand in the middle of the room facing one side of the room. Make a fist and rotate your right arm in front of you. Rotate your arm in front of you in a clockwise direction. Ask the participants whether your arm is moving in the clockwise direction or counterclockwise direction. Different people will respond differently depending on their position in front of you or behind your back.

Jolt 4
Dear John

Punctuation can make a big difference in the meaning of a sentence. Take for example the two sentences below that have vastly different meanings as a result of comma and colon placement:

Woman, without her man, is nothing.
Woman: Without her, man is nothing.

We have incorporated a few other common examples of the power of punctuation in this jolt. You can find many others to use in this jolt if you wish through a simple search of the Internet.

 ## Synopsis

Participants are asked to correct the punctuation in a "Dear John" letter distributed by the facilitator and then work though two additional handouts that demonstrate clearly how details matter.

 ## Purpose

- To demonstrate the importance of paying attention to small details

 ## Training Topics

- Mindfulness
- Communication

 ## Participants

- One or more
- The best group size is 12 to 20 participants divided into teams

 ## Time

- 3 minutes for the activity
- 5 to 10 minutes for debriefing

Handouts

- "Dear John" letter without punctuation (Handout 1)
- Two versions of the "Dear John" letter with punctuation (Handouts 2 and 3)

 Flow

Distribute copies of Handout 1 to each participant.

Organize teams. Divide participants into teams of two to five members each.

Give instructions. Ask the participants to read the handout and add suitable punctuation marks to make the meaning clear. Emphasize that changing the order of the words is not permitted and that they may not add or delete any of the words in the letter. Wait a few minutes for each participant to complete work on the punctuation activity.

Distribute copies of the punctuated versions. After passing out Handouts 2 and 3, give the participants a few minutes to read the two versions before asking a few volunteers to read the two versions of the letters with appropriate pauses and inflection to convey the two different meanings. Emphasize how the meaning completely changed between the two versions.

 Debriefing

Debrief participants. Ask the participants whether they can think of any examples when the punctuation of printed words or the tone of the spoken word has drastically changed the intended meaning.

 Learning Points

1. How you use words is often the most important factor in determining meaning.
2. Small details **do** make big difference.

 Variation

You want more relevant text? Replace the supplied handouts with a business memo you create that delivers an equally dramatic example of the power of punctuation. Better yet, assign this challenge to the participants as a follow-up activity.

Dear John Handout 1

Instructions: Punctuate this letter to make its meaning clear.

dear john i want a man who knows what love is all

about you are generous kind thoughtful people who

are not like you admit to being useless and inferior

you have ruined me for other men i yearn for you

i have no feeling whatsoever when were apart i can

be forever happy will you let me be yours gloria

Dear John Handout 2: Punctuated Letter (Version 1)

Dear John,

I want a man who knows what love is all about. You are generous, kind, thoughtful. People who are not like you admit to being useless and inferior. You have ruined me for other men. I yearn for you. I have no feeling whatsoever when we're apart. I can be forever happy—will you let me be yours?

Gloria

Dear John:

I want a man who knows what love is. All about you

are generous, kind, thoughtful people who are not

like you. Admit to being useless and inferior. You

have ruined me. For other men, I yearn. For you,

I have no feeling whatsoever. When we're apart,

I can be forever happy. Will you let me be?

Yours,
Gloria

Jolt 5
Decode

We are all conditioned to cooperate within teams and to compete against other teams. Yet sometimes a better strategy is to not only cooperate within our own team but to cooperate with other teams for better results.

 ## Synopsis

Participants are asked to organize themselves into teams and to decode a cryptogram. Team members naturally assume that they are competing with the other teams in order to "win." What the participants learn during the activity is that the best strategy would have been cooperation between the individual teams, rather than competition.

 ## Purpose

- To explore the effectiveness cooperation among groups of teams

 ## Caution

Don't let decoding the cryptogram be the focus of the session (even though the participants may find solving the puzzle to be very engaging). Make sure everyone is engrossed in the discussion during the debriefing.

 ## Training Topics

- Teamwork
- Cooperation
- Competition

 ## Participants

- Eight or more
- The recommended number of game participants is 15 to 30

Time

- 5 minutes for the activity
- 10 to 15 minutes for debriefing

Handouts

- Handout 1: Instruction Sheet (one copy for each player)
- Handout 2: Cryptogram (one copy for each player)
- Handout 3: Answer Key (one copy for the facilitator)

Equipment

- Countdown timer
- Whistle

Flow

Organize teams. Divide the participants into teams of four to seven members each. Seat each team around a table.

Brief participants. Distribute copies of the Instruction Sheet (Handout 1) and ask how many participants have any experience solving cryptogram puzzles. Briefly explain what a cryptogram is (using the information from the handout). Explain that all teams will be tasked with solving a cryptogram.

Explain time limits and the scoring system. Tell the participants that any team that correctly and completely solves the cryptogram within 2 minutes, will earn 200 points. Note that if a team takes more than 2 minutes but less than 3 minutes, then that team will earn 50 points.

Explain coaching support. Tell the participants that you will offer one-time help by decoding *any single word* in the distributed cryptogram. The team members collectively must select the word for decoding and send a representative to you for this coaching support.

Distribute the cryptogram. Place enough copies of the cryptogram (Handout 2) for each team member face down in the center of each table.

Begin the puzzle-solving activity. Set your timer for 2 minutes and ask the teams to distribute the cryptogram in the groups and to begin decoding the handout. Remind the participants of your coaching support.

Conclude the session. If any team has completely and correctly decoded the message before the 2-minute time limit, award the 200 points. At the end of 2 minutes, announce the time and set the timer for another minute. At the end of 3 minutes, announce the end of the session. Read aloud the correct solution given in Handout 3, even if all the teams have not yet solved the cryptogram.

Debriefing

Use selected questions from the following list to encourage discussion:

- *What would have been the best strategy for rapidly decoding the puzzle?*
- *If each team had asked the facilitator to decode a different word, and shared this information with the other teams, it would have been easier for all team to decode the cryptogram. Did anyone think of this idea? Did you share this idea with the other members of your team? Why or why not?*
- *Why do you think most teams don't use a cooperative strategy?*
- *Have you ever been in a situation in which teams unnecessarily competed with each other? Why did this happen?*

Learning Points

1. In situations that involve multiple teams, each team naturally assumes that their team is in competition with all the other teams in the group.
2. Cooperation among teams (rather than competition) often produces better and more effective results.

Variations

Don't have enough participants? You can play the game among with individuals. Ask each participant to solve the cryptogram and adapt the rules used for teams to fit individual play. We have played this game with just two people and decoded three words for each player to compensate for the lack of team members.

Do you have a group of non-English speakers? Use a different type of puzzle. We have used Sudoku puzzles and provided the position of half-a-dozen additional numbers as coaching support.

You don't want to decode words to help the teams? Here's an alternative way of giving clues: Give team member the regular English letters that are represented by two cryptic letters.

Field Notes

It is possible for the teams to decode the message within 2 minutes if they cooperate with each other. Most groups fail because they waste time in figuring out—and agreeing on—a cooperative strategy. Without this type of strategy (and with a single word decoded), teams need 4 or 5 minutes to decode the message. By the way, even without clues, an experienced cryptographer can decode the message in 2 to 3 minutes.

Decode Handout 1: Instruction Sheet

You are probably familiar with codes and cryptograms from your childhood days. In a cryptogram, each letter in the message is replaced by another letter of the alphabet. For example,

LET THE GAMES BEGIN!

becomes this cryptogram:

YZF FOZ JUKZH CZJVQ!

In the cryptogram Y replaces L, Z replaces E, F replaces T, and so on. Notice that the same letter substitutions are used throughout this cryptogram: Every E in the sentence is replaced by a Z, and every T is replaced by an F.

A New Cryptogram
Your team will be asked to solve a new cryptogram. This puzzle uses a different scheme for letter substitutions.

Scoring System
If a team solves the cryptogram within 2 minutes, the team receives 200 points.

If a team takes more than 2 minutes but less than 3 minutes, the team receives 50 points.

Decode Handout 2: Cryptogram

ISV'B JZZXYH BPJB BPH SVQE UJE

\- -'- - - - - - - - - - - - - - - - - - - -

BS UCV CZ BS FSYTHBH. ZSYHBCYHZ

\- - - - - - - - - - - - - - -. - - - - - - - -

BPH AHZB UJE BS UCV CZ BS

\- - - - - - - - - - - - - - - - - - -

FSSTHWJBH UCBP SBPHWZ.

\- - - - - - - - - - - - - - - - - -.

Decode Handout 3: Answer Sheet

ISV'B	JZZXYH	BPJB	BPH	SVQE	UJE
DON'T	ASSUME	THAT	THE	ONLY	WAY

BS	UCV	CZ	BS	FSYTHBH.	ZSYHBCYHZ
TO	WIN	IS	TO	COMPETE.	SOMETIMES

BPH	AHZB	UJE	BS	UCV	CZ	BS
THE	BEST	WAY	TO	WIN	IS	TO

FSSTHWJBH	UCBP	SBPHWZ.
COOPERATE	WITH	OTHERS.

Jolt 6
Dollar Auction

This activity, originally designed by the economist Martin Shubik, is technically a non-zero-sum sequential game. It illustrates how a series of rational choices may ultimately lead you to make irrational decisions. We use this simplified and speeded-up version as a jolt to illustrate a variety of interpersonal concepts.

Synopsis

Participants take part in an auction for a single dollar bill and follow an unusual bidding scenario. At the end of the auction, both the highest and second-highest bidders are declared the winners. Like a traditional auction, the highest bidder receives the prize (the dollar bill). Unlike other auctions, the second-highest bidder must still pay the bid amount as well. The surprising lesson (and conundrum for the bidders) is that paying *more* for the dollar actually *saves* money.

Purpose

- To explore factors related to the escalation of interpersonal conflicts

Training Topics

- Critical thinking
- Addiction
- Escalation

Participants

- Two or more
- The best game involves 10 to 30 participants

Time

- 3 to 5 minutes for the auction
- 7 to 15 minutes for debriefing

Supplies

- A dollar bill

Caution

This game has the potential to last longer than is needed to make the desired point. As the "auctioneer" you should watch the time and subtly bring the activity to a close when you feel the purpose has been achieved.

Flow

Brief the participants. Hold up a dollar bill and explain that you will auction it off. Ask the participants to listen carefully as you explain the rules. Here are some rule notes that you can use for your explanation:

- *The opening bid is 50 cents and all subsequent bids must be in 10-cent increments*
- *You cannot skip any increment. (For example, after someone bids 60 cents, you can't jump to 80 cents.)*
- *When the bidding stops, the highest bidder must pay the bid amount to the auctioneer and then will receive the dollar.*
- *The second-highest bidder must also pay his or her bid amount—but the second-highest bidder will receive nothing in return. (For example, if at the end of the auction one participant [Diane] bids 80 cents for the dollar but is beat out by another participant [Jonathan] who has bid 90 cents, then Jonathan pays 90 cents and gets the dollar while Diane pays her 80 cents and gets nothing in return.)*

Start the auction. Call for the opening bid of 50 cents. Our experience is that the first few bids clump together immediately after the opening bid. Bids on the dollar generally slow down around 80 cents and only two participants emerge from the competition.

Encourage continuous bidding. After someone bids 90 cents, wait for a moment to see whether momentum carries the two bidders forward. If you sense a pause in the bidding, remind the participant who made the 80-cent bid (the second-highest bid amount) that the rules do not prohibit bids of a dollar or more. Usually the bidders figure out that bidding more than a dollar saves money (!). If an explanation is needed, then provide the following financial advice to the second-highest bidder:

- *If you stop now, you lose 80 cents. But if you bid a dollar, you lose nothing. You pay a dollar and get back a dollar.*

Conclude the auction. Stop when one bidder gives up. Collect the money from the top two bidders and give the dollar bill to the highest bidder. (Return the money to the bidders after the debriefing discussion, but for now you should maintain the illusion that you are serious.)

Debriefing

This jolt usually leads to a lengthy reflection on various aspects of human behavior. Here are some sample questions that you may use for your debriefing discussion:

- *How do you think the highest bidder feels about the activity?*
- *How do you think the second-highest bidder feels about the activity?*
- *How do you think the spectators feel about the bidders' behavior?*
- *What made some participants begin bidding initially?*
- *Why did some people not participate in the bidding?*
- *Here's a key question: Why did some people bid more than a dollar for a dollar?*
- *Does this activity remind you of events in your workplace?*
- *How does the activity reflect escalation of a conflict between two people?*
- *How does this activity simulate addiction?*
- *What would have happened if we auctioned $100 with $50 as the starting bid and $10 increments?*
- *What would have happened if the bidding was among teams instead of individuals?*

Learning Points

1. Curiosity often drives people to take risks.
2. Most contests eventually narrow down to two competitors.
3. Competition often drives people to lose perspective. In the case of this jolt, the competitive nature leads participants to:
   a. Bid beyond the true value of a dollar because they don't want to lose
   b. Not consider forming a coalition to split their losses
4. In most auctions, the auctioneer is the only person who profits.

Variations

Do you want to increase the tension? After the bid reaches $1.50, announce a new rule that permits bidding in any increments as long as it is *more* than 10 cents.

Do you think that $1 does not mean much in this economy? Conduct a $10 auction with a $5 opening bid and $1 increments.

Field Notes

We have conducted this activity around the world (in India, Switzerland, Japan, Indonesia, the United Kingdom, and Singapore) using local currency. The results are remarkably similar, suggesting some universal principles of human behavior.

In case you are curious, the highest bid we ever elicited with this activity was $67. Part of the reason might have been our intention to contribute all profits to charity.

We have conducted this auction literally thousands of times. While our sampling might be limited, we have not noticed consistent trends related to age, gender, and cultural differences.

Jolts! Activities to Wake Up and Engage Your Participants

Jolt 7
Don't Lift the Pen

This jolt uses two quick puzzles to teach some important principles about problem solving.

 ## Synopsis

The facilitator begins by drawing two concentric circles (a circle within a circle) on a flip chart with a line running through the center of both circles. Participants are asked to replicate the drawing using blank sheets of paper and pens provided by the facilitator. The exercise appears easy until the participants learn about restrictions on how the drawing must be done: Participants are not allowed to lift their pens off the paper once the drawing begins and cannot retrace any lines.

 ## Purpose

- To explore how thinking outside the box helps solve problems and how different strategies may be needed to solve problems that may appear similar

 ## Training Topics

- Problem solving
- Creative thinking

 ## Participants

- One or more
- This activity is intended for individuals working independently

 ## Time

- 3 minutes for the activity
- 5 to 10 minutes for debriefing

Supplies

- Paper
- Pen or pencils
- Flip chart
- Felt-tipped markers

Preparation

Read the instructions and practice drawing the pictures on a flip chart before you present this jolt.

Flow

Present the first graphic. Draw two concentric circles on your flip chart and complete the drawing with a straight line cutting through the center. Make sure that everyone can see the finished figure.

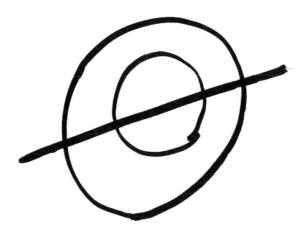

Explain the challenge. Ensure that each participant has a blank piece of paper and a pen. Ask the participants to draw a picture similar to the one on the flip chart and tell them that they have to complete this task *without lifting their pens off the paper and without retracing any lines.*

Show how to do it. Pause for about a minute while the participants try to complete the task and observe what everyone is doing. If someone does successfully complete the task, offer congratulations and ask the person to demonstrate how to complete the drawing on another sheet of flip-chart paper. If no one completes the task successfully, use the picture below to demonstrate. (In this picture, we have exaggerated the gaps to show the path your line should take.)

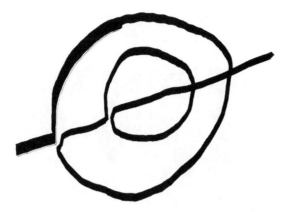

Draw a new figure. On another sheet of flip-chart paper, draw two concentric circles, like those shown below:

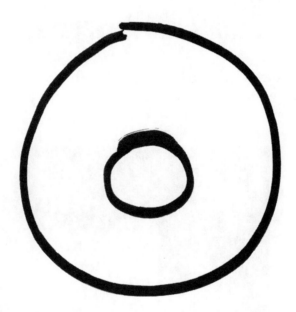

Present the second challenge. Ask participants to draw two concentric circles, similar to the ones on the flip chart, but again without lifting their pens off the paper and without retracing any lines.

Pause for about a minute. Observe the progress of the participants and congratulate those who successfully complete the task.

Demonstrate how to do the drawing. Refer to the next drawing to learn how to complete the task:

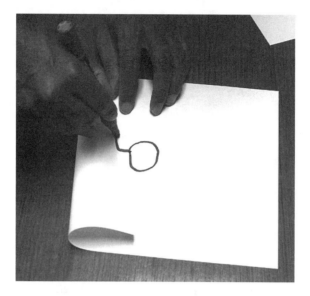

Begin by drawing the smaller circle. Then fold the bottom part of the paper so the back of the sheet touches the bottom of the circle. Without lifting the pen, draw a line away from the circle on the back of the paper as shown below.

After the line reaches a suitable distance away from the smaller circle, move the tip of the pen to the front of the sheet. Release the folded part of the flip chart paper and draw the outer circle to complete the task.

Debriefing

Conduct a debriefing discussion that focuses on how this activity illustrates creative problem solving. Ask questions that illustrate the learning points below.

Learning Points

1. Tasks that appear to be impossible at first may be accomplished by thinking outside the box.
2. Sometimes entirely different approaches are needed to solve very similar problems.

Jolt 8
Double Talk

Participants at a training session or in meetings are often preoccupied with other important things in their lives. Here's a simple jolt to wake them up.

 ## Synopsis

A pair of participants demonstrates the impact of distraction through role play as one participant endeavors to listen to your lecture while the other participant whispers distracting thoughts. At the end of the activity, neither of the participants can recall the content of your lecture.

 ## Purpose

- To experience the effects of self-talk

 ## Training Topic

- Mindfulness

 ## Participants

- Two or more

 ## Time

- 4 minutes for the activity
- 5 to 10 minutes for debriefing

 ## Flow

Organize pairs. Ask participants to pair themselves up. In each pair, ask the taller participant to assume the role of a listener and the other participant to become the IV. Announce that you will explain what the acronym stands for later.

Assign the task to IVs. Explain that IVs are to sit close to the listeners and to whisper a string of disconnected distracting thoughts that likely occupy the minds of most listeners.

Add details. Recommend that the IVs use topics that are highly interesting (*Should I buy a lottery ticket?*) or disturbing (*What if the company decides to right size again?*) or bothersome (*Did I turn the stove off this morning?*) or intriguing (*What exactly does Sheila see in him?*) or guilt-provoking (*I forgot Doug's birthday again!*). Also suggest that the IVs should use first-person singular and run-on sentences in a stream-of-consciousness mode.

Start a lecture. Give a short, fact-filled presentation on some dry topic. Simultaneously ask the IVs to begin whispering. Continue with this combined activity for 2 to 3 minutes.

Stop your lecture. Thank the IVs for their imaginative contributions and ask them to stop whispering. Ask the listeners the jot down some of the words, ideas, and topics mentioned by the IV. Pause for a minute.

Test everyone. Ask a series of short-answer questions based on the content of your lecture. Ask all participants (both listeners and IVs) to raise their hands if they know the answers.

Debriefing

Point out that the listening of everyone in the room was impacted and that both listeners and whisperers missed some important points in your presentation.

Explain that IV stands for the Inner Voice and that the whispers simulate self-talk and ruminations. Conduct a quick survey to find out how many participants are currently having a self-talk session. Continue with a discussion to elicit the point that this internal dialogue reduces learning effectiveness. Ask the participants to brainstorm techniques for stopping distracting self-talk and focusing on what others are saying.

Variations

Want everyone to experience the role of an IV? Repeat the activity with the players switching roles.

Want to be more dramatic? Form groups of three and assign two IVs (one for each ear) to each listener.

Jolt 9
Double Your Money

Prisoner's Dilemma is a classic game that is based on an experimental design that explores cooperation and competition. You may learn more about this game by conducting an online search. This jolt is based on this classic Prisoner's Dilemma activity—and it may cost you $80.

 ## Synopsis

Participants have the opportunity to double their money and explore the consequences of different strategies related to keeping or giving away money.

 ## Purpose

- To explore internal and external factors that affect collaboration

 ## Training Topics

- Cooperation
- Trust

 ## Participants

- Any number
- The activity requires you to bring two "volunteers" to the front of the room. Initially, other participants watch the action, but later everyone has the opportunity to give advice to these two participants.

 ## Time

- 3 minutes for the activity
- 10 to 15 minutes for debriefing

Supplies

- $40 in cash, preferably in $1 bills
- Two envelopes

Caution

The two players brought to the front will be on the spot and under peer pressure. Not all the participants will approve of the two players' decisions, so be careful whom you select for the activity. During debriefing emphasize that the players made decisions under contrived conditions and that these decisions are unlikely to represent their typical behaviors under normal circumstances.

Flow

Select two participants. Ask the selected participants (preferably a man and a woman and someone you know) to come to the front of the room. Ask one participant to stand on your right and the other person to stand on your left.

Give $20 to each participant. Give each participant 20 $1 bills. Do it with some fanfare to attract the attention of the other participants.

Give an envelope to each player. Tell the players that they can put as much of the $20 in the envelope as they wish—and that when this is done to give the envelope to the other player.

Explain the details. Use your own words to clarify the rules of the game:

Place as much of the $20 in the envelope as you want before giving the envelope to the other player. However, once you have given the envelope to the other player, you cannot get the money back.

That means you may place all $20 in the envelope and give it the other player or you may choose to place $5 in the envelope and put the remaining $15 in your pocket. Or you may choose to deliver an empty envelope to the other player and keep all the money.

Explain the doubling principle. Use your own words to convey this message:

Please listen carefully to this important piece of information: After you have exchanged the envelopes, I will open each of them and double the money inside. This bonus money belongs to the person who received the envelope. For example, if you gave $20 to the other player, I will give her another $20, making the total $40. If you gave an empty envelope to the other person, I will match it giving the player nothing more. If you gave the player $5, I will add another $5 to the total The extra money you receive depends on the action of the other player. Keep this doubling principle in mind when you decide how much money you want to place inside the envelope.

Ask the two players to talk to other participants. Invite the other participants to help the players make their decisions by saying something like:

Let's tap into the wisdom of the crowd. I will wait for 2 minutes while you have conversations with your friends in the audience. Get as many suggestions as you want. These suggestions may contradict each other and only you have to make the final decision about how much money to put inside the envelope.

Pause while the two players mingle with the other participants.

Exchange the envelopes. At the end of 2 minutes, bring the two players back to the front of the room. Ask them turn their backs to each other. Ask them to secretly place the money they want to give to the other participant in the envelope. Ask each player to hide the rest of the $20 in his or her pocket or purse. Ask the two players to exchange their envelopes.

Double the money. Go to one of the players and take the envelope he or she received from the other player. Build up a little bit of suspense with a dramatic envelope opening. Count the money inside (if any) and match the amount of dollars as promised from your pocket. Give the new packet of cash to the player and repeat the procedure with the other player.

Debriefing

Explain this activity is a variation of the classic Prisoner's Dilemma game that explores competition and collaboration between two players. Conduct a debriefing discussion among all participants to explore collaboration and competition. Ask questions similar to these:

- *What is your reaction to the process and outcome of this activity?*
- *What interesting things did you observe during the activity?*
- *What did you learn from this activity?*
- *How do the events in this activity reflect the events in your workplace?*

Ask the two participants who played the game these questions. Let other participants react to their responses:

- *What different types of suggestions did you get from the audience members?*
- *Which suggestion did you choose to implement? Why did you choose it?*

Ask "what if?" questions. This activity becomes exciting when the two players behave in different ways. In most situations, however, this jolt may produce bland results because both players simply place the entire $20 in the envelope. You may expand the range of learning by posing and discussing the following types of "what-if?" questions:

- *What if the two players had to use their own money (up to $20) instead of using the money I gave them?*

- *What if each player was given $500 instead of $20?*
- *What if no money was given to the players but they were told to place their own money—up to $500—in the envelopes?*
- *What if the activity involved two teams (whose members make joint decisions) instead of two individuals?*
- *What if the activity involved two people who have never met before? What if the two players had known each other for a long time?*
- *How would gender differences affect this activity? What if both players were women? What if they were both men? What if the activity involved one man and one woman?*
- *How would generational differences affect the players' decisions and actions? What If they were college students? What if they were high school students?*
- *What if the two players came from different countries and different cultures?*
- *What if no audience members were observing this event?*
- *What if this activity was broadcast on network TV?*
- *What if the amounts in the envelopes were not revealed to the audience members and the final settlements were made only after everyone left the session?*
- *What if this activity was conducted on the Internet and the true identities of the players were never revealed?*
- *What if each player was assigned one or two advisors?*
- *What if both players exchanged empty envelopes? What if they both exchanged $20? What if one player gave an empty envelope and other gave $20?*
- *What if the two players had a day to think about how much money they wanted to put in the envelopes? What if the players had to make their decisions in 30 seconds?*
- *What if the players were accountants and they conducted a cost-benefit analysis before deciding how much money to place in the envelope?*

 Learning Points

1. Financial outcomes influence the way people behave.
2. Spectators affect the way that decisions are made.
3. Decisions about cooperation and competition bring out the full range of human tendency toward gullibility and paranoia.
4. Getting consensus on any decision in a group situation is difficult.

 Field Notes

Bad news: Typical players put the $20 inside the envelopes, which forces you to double the money and spend $80. *Good news:* After the session, typical players return the money to you. I have no recommendations about whether you should take the money back or let the players keep it. (I took the money back.)

The use of U.S. currency in the description above is for our convenience. Obviously, international readers would use equivalent money in the local currency.

Jolt 10
Draw a Hand

Very often, people act on the basis of their mental pictures rather than what they see in the outside world. This jolt emphasizes our dependence on internal models.

 ## Synopsis

Participants are asked to draw a picture of a hand. When the task is completed, the facilitator points out that very few of the participants used their own hands or the hands of others to draw their pictures.

 ## Purpose

- To experience how mental models shape our activities

 ## Training Topics

- Mindfulness
- Stereotyping

 ## Participants

- One or more

 ## Time

- 2 minutes for the activity
- 3 to 5 minutes for debriefing

 ## Supplies

- Index cards
- Pens or pencils

Preparation

To speed up the process, place an index card and a pencil on each seat before the participants arrive

 Flow

Give instructions. Ask the participants to use the index card and pencil to draw a picture of a hand and set a time limit of 45 seconds. Pause while participants complete this task.

   Conclude the activity. Announce the end of the activity after 45 seconds even if some of the artists are still working on their masterpieces.

 Debriefing

Ask how many participants looked at their hands or their neighbors' hands to draw the picture. Note that very few participants took advantage of that opportunity. Present this major learning point in your own words:

   Most of us don't look at reality, even though it is right in front of us. That is because we prefer to work with a mental model. We think with these mental models and we frequently base our performance on them. Psychologists call the act of creating mental models generalization, abstraction, concept acquisition, or stereotyping.

   It does not matter if you draw a picture of a hand based on your mental model. However, it does matter if you come up with a company policy based on your mental model of a female employee or an employee of Asian origin. This is because your mental model could be distorted and, therefore, your policy may not produce the intended effect on the wide range of people it is supposed to affect.

 Learning Points

1. We act upon mental models instead of reality.
2. Our mental models frequently distort reality and may result in unrealistic decisions.

 Variation

You think that drawing hands is a little clichéd? Ask your participants to draw a picture of a shoe or a handbag.

Follow-Up Jolt

You may follow up with Jolt 11, Draw a Tree, since this jolt uses a similar task and emphasizes a related concept.

Jolt 11
Draw a Tree

*O*ut of sight, out of mind. As this familiar saying suggests, we tend to ignore things that we cannot see, even when they are very important.

 ## Synopsis

Participants are asked draw a tree, but most will not draw the roots as part of the tree. As the facilitator, you point out the importance of roots and connect the significance of the omission of the tree's roots to the learning point of paying attention to all parts of a system.

 ## Purpose

- To stress the importance of infrastructure and support systems not immediately visible

 ## Training Topics

- Critical thinking
- Mindfulness

 ## Participants

- One or more

 ## Time

- 2 minutes for the activity
- 5 to 10 minutes for debriefing

 ## Supplies

- Index cards
- Pens or pencils

Preparation

Before the participants arrive, leave an index card and pencil on the seats for use during the activity.

Flow

Give instructions. Ask the participants to draw tree on the index cards you provided. Set a time limit of 45 seconds. Explain that the drawing can be realistic or abstract and that the critical requirement is that the drawing be completed within the 45-second time limit.

    Conclude the activity. At the end of 45 seconds announce the end of the activity.

Debriefing

Ask participants to look at their drawings and raise their hands if their drawing shows roots. You are likely to find that most did not include the root system in their rendering of a tree. Present the following learning point in your own words:

- *All of your trees likely have trunks and branches and leaves. But most of them do not have roots.*

- *So what is holding up the trees without the root system? How do your trees get water and nutrition?*

- *Do you agree that the root system is an important part of tree? Why did you leave out the root system? Was it because you usually don't see the roots?*

    Ask participants to suggest other things we habitually ignore just because these important support elements are not visible. Use the example of the current training session and ask the participants to identify the people behind the scenes who contribute to the success of the training experience.

    Ask participants to discuss the possible dangers of neglecting what we cannot immediately see. Brainstorm some techniques for preventing this habit.

Learning Points

1. We tend to ignore things that are not clearly visible.
2. Very often the things we choose to ignore play a important role in our success.

Follow-Up

If you want to extend this jolt, you can pair it with Jolt 10, Draw a Hand, which uses a similar drawing approach and makes a related learning point.

Jolt 12
Ears for Smiley

Job performance is increased if guidance is provided before an activity and feedback is given after an activity. However, very few employees ask for guidance and feedback. This jolt increases both the awareness of the vital role of feedback and the willingness of the participants to ask for and receive useful feedback.

 ## Synopsis

Participants are asked to choose partners for this role-play activity. The facilitator assigns the role of the manager to one partner and the role of the employee to the other. The partners identified as employees are asked to close their eyes and to draw the familiar smiley face icon with a circular face, two dots for eyes, a curved smiling line for a mouth, and a pair of ears. Participants discover that the best smiley faces with ears were drawn by participants who were willing to ask for guidance.

 ## Purpose

- To demonstrate the importance of asking for guidance and feedback

 ## Training Topics

- Guidance
- Feedback
- Leadership

 ## Participants

- Two and more
- The best number of participants is 8 to 20

 ## Time

- 5 minutes for the activity
- 8 to 10 minutes for the debriefing

Supplies

- Pen or pencils
- Paper
- Whistle

Flow

Assign roles. Ask the participants to pair up. In each pair, one participant takes on the role of a manager and the other an employee. Distribute a blank sheet of paper to each employee.

Give initial instructions. Provide the following instructions in your own words:

Managers, your task is to make sure that the employee you are managing follows my instructions.

Employees, your task is to draw a picture of a smiley face. Please don't begin until I complete all my instructions. Your smiley should have a circular face, two dots for the eyes, and a curved line for a smiling mouth.

*Here's an important constraint to remember for this activity: You must draw the picture with your **eyes closed**. So please close your eyes now and keep them closed. Managers, make sure that your employees follow the restriction that their eyes must be closed throughout this activity.*

*Employees, **when I say go you can begin your drawing**. You have 30 seconds to draw your smiley.*

Pause while the employees complete the task. At the end of 30 seconds blow your whistle and ask the employees to stop.

Give additional instructions. Continue with these instructions, again in your own words:

Employees, please keep your eyes closed. I have some additional instructions for you.

First, please transfer your pen or pencil to your other hand. Don't open your eyes.

Now, I'd like you to add a pair of ears to your smiley face.

*OK, transfer your pen or pencil back to your preferred hand and draw the two ears. Please begin now. **You have 30 seconds.***

Conclude the activity. Wait for the employee partners to complete the task. Blow your whistle and ask the employees to open their eyes to inspect their smiley faces. Invite them to hold them up their work for others to see.

Most smiley faces are likely to have misplaced ears. Wait while the participants laugh at their efforts.

Debriefing

The main learning point of this jolt is that performance is improved if people seek guidance and feedback. Drive home this point with questions like this:

- *Most of us know the importance of asking for guidance and feedback. How many of you asked your managers to give you guidance and feedback while you were drawing your smiley faces?*

Congratulate any employees who asked for guidance and feedback and ask these participants to hold up their smiley faces. Continue with the debriefing using your own version of this suggested script:

> *Some of you may feel that you must not ask a manager for guidance and feedback. Actually, you should ask for feedback from everybody: your managers, your subordinates, your coworkers, your significant others, your children, your customers, your friends, and your enemies. You should ask for guidance and feedback at all times. You should be constantly asking yourself, "Who can I ask for guidance and feedback right now?"*
>
> *When should you ask for guidance and feedback? Should you have drawn the ears and then asked your manager whether you placed them in the appropriate locations? Or should you have pointed to some location and asked your manager whether it is an appropriate location for the right ear?*

Note that managers have a responsibility to provide useful guidance and feedback. Convey this point with debriefing questions like these:

- *How many managers provided guidance and feedback to your employees? Why didn't the majority of you provide the employee with guidance and feedback?*
- *Which is better: Providing guidance before the employee begins an activity or feedback after the employee completes the activity?*
- *How much guidance and feedback do you think is appropriate? What are the consequences of too much or too little feedback?*

 Learning Points

1. As an employee or learner you should take every opportunity to ask for guidance and feedback.
2. As a manager or leader you should take every opportunity to offer appropriate guidance and feedback.

 Variation

Do you find drawing smiley faces trivial? You can ask the "employees" to draw a small diagram that is relevant to their jobs or draw the organization's logo.

Jolt 13
Enjoy and Learn

Use this jolt to re-engage your participants in the training session. You can introduce the jolt at any time to encourage your training participants to choose to be present and engaged.

 ## Synopsis

You ask the participants to point to the person they think is enjoying and learning the most from the training session. After pretending to collect data in order to choose the participant enjoying the session the most and promising to point out the winner of the class poll, you point out a surprising choice—you are the one who is enjoying the session and learning the most from it.

 ## Purpose

- To choose to enjoy and learn from the training session

 ## Training Topic

- Motivation

 ## Participants

- One or more participants

 ## Time

- 2 minutes for the activity
- 3 to 10 minutes for the debriefing

Flow

Make a declaration. At some time during the first half-hour of a workshop (or the first 10 minutes of a presentation), pause suddenly as if struck by a startling epiphany. Make the following statement in your own words:

> *I have been carefully observing everyone's behaviors and reading the minds of everyone in the room. I have analyzed the data and discovered the person who is going to learn the most from this training session and enjoy it the most.*

Invite predictions from participants. Ask everyone to look around and locate the person who is going to learn the most and enjoy the most from your session or presentation. Count to three and ask participants to point to this person.

Collect data. Pause briefly and count "One, two, three." Take a quick look at the different people who are being pointed out. Also make a note of participants (if any) who point to themselves.

Reveal your selection. Announce that participants' choices are definitely close to your choice. With some dramatic flair, say you are going to point out the one person who will enjoy the session the most and learn the most. Continue to build up some suspense. Count to three once again and point to—yourself.

 Debriefing

Give this pep talk, in your own words:

> *I am going to enjoy this workshop and I am going to learn the most. I have the choice about what I want to do and how I want to feel. I set high expectations and choose to behave in ways that will enable me to transform these expectations into reality.*
>
> *You too have the choice. I hope you will choose to behave in ways that makes this the most enjoyable and the most useful training experience you ever had.*
>
> *Think about that for a few moments.*

Pause for about 20 seconds and return to what you were doing before this jolt interlude.

 Learning Point

1. If you set high expectations of how you want to feel and what you want to achieve, you can align your activities appropriately.

Jolt 14
Excited

Unlike most of the other jolts in this book, this one requires at least fifteen people. You will need seven participants to come to the front of the room to perform a task while the remaining participants yell out instructions.

Synopsis

Seven volunteer participants are invited to come to the front of the room and form a straight line. The facilitator hands out large cards to the participants, each card displaying a different letter printed in large, bold type. The facilitator instructs the rest of the participants to shout suggestions on how to rearrange the volunteers and their letters to spell a word.

Purpose

- To identify factors that make a task exciting

Training Topic

- Motivation

Participants

- Fifteen or more participants

Time

- 3 to 5 minutes for the activity
- 5 to 10 minutes for debriefing

Supplies

- Prepare seven large cards on index stock, one with each of these letters written in bold: C D E E I T X

Flow

Call for volunteers. Ask seven people from the group to come to the front of the room and form a straight line facing the rest of the participants.

Distribute the letter cards. Give each volunteer one letter card and instruct everyone to hold their letters up high so that the others can read them easily.

Give instructions. Explain that the letters spell a seven-letter English word. Ask the other participants to rearrange the position of the volunteers in the line so that the cards they are holding spell the correct word. Encourage the audience to call out their suggestions and give an example of how to request changes in the word order. For example, you might suggest the following; "One of the people with the letter E, please move to the beginning of the word. The person with the letter D, move to the end."

Provide clues. Tell those holding the letters to follow the instructions from the audience. (The letters spell the word "EXCITED.") You may give some hints to speed up the process, if necessary.

Conclude the activity. When the word is correctly formed, ask the participants to read the solution out loud on the count of three. Thank the volunteer letter holders, collect the letter cards, and send the volunteers back to their seats. Lead a round of applause for the entire group for rapidly solving the puzzle.

Debriefing

Begin the debriefing by asking the group if the activity was exciting. Ask the participants to identify what made the activity so exciting. Use appropriate probing questions to elicit the following responses from your participants:

- *The activity was brief.*
- *The activity was unexpected.*
- *Everybody was invited to participate in the activity, but nobody was forced to participate.*
- *The activity was intellectually stimulating.*
- *Participants were yelling out their directions in a playfully chaotic fashion.*
- *Participants were not taking turns and behaving politely.*
- *It was a group challenge rather than an individual challenge.*
- *It was a cooperative activity.*
- *The feedback was immediate.*
- *The letter holders enjoyed being the center of attention.*
- *Members of the audience enjoyed their power to push people around.*
- *There was a sense of urgency, even though there was no time limit.*

Ask participants to brainstorm how these ideas can be applied to increase the excitement level of everyday activities.

Learning Points

1. Use of interactive techniques increases the motivation level to complete or follow through with any task.
2. Empowering participants to make their own decisions results in increased learning.

Field Notes

Make sure that the letter cards you make can withstand rough handling. If you have the time and resources, laminate the cards.

Jolt 15
First Touch

Use this jolt to explore opportunities for win-win solutions among participants.

 ## Synopsis

Two participants are asked to hold their index fingers six inches above a "Rule Sheet" that the facilitator has placed on the table. The winner or loser of the game is determined by the person whose index finger touches the rule sheet first during the course of the game.

 ## Purpose

- To explore the reasons why players do not naturally gravitate toward strategies that ensure mutual victory

 ## Training Topics

- Negotiation
- Problem solving
- Cooperation

 ## Participants

- Three or more, divided into groups of three

 ## Time

- 3 minutes for the activity
- 5 to 15 minutes for debriefing

 ## Handout

- One copy of a the First Touch Rule Sheet for each group

Flow

Form groups. Ask participants to organize themselves into groups of three. Appoint one person in each group to be the Rule Sheet Referee and give that appointee a copy of the Rule Sheet.

Brief the participants. Explain that the game is very simple and the two simple rules for winning (or losing) are printed on the Rule Sheet.

Explain the responsibilities of the Rule Sheet to the Referee in each group. Tell the referee that his or her job, in addition to placing the Rule Sheet on the table with the printed side up, is to observe the behavior of the other two players.

Give instructions to the players. Ask the two players in each group to extend their right index fingers and each hold that finger approximately six inches above the surface of the Rule Sheet while pointing to the rules.

Read the rules. Ask participants to read and repeat the two rules on the Rule Sheet: *You win if you get the other person's right index finger to touch the Rule Sheet first. You lose if your right index finger touches the Rule Sheet first.*

Conduct the game. Say, "Let the game begin!" Walk among the different groups and observe what the players are doing. Make a mental note of any interesting strategy.

Conclude the game. After about 2 minutes or whenever the majority of players have completed the task, stop the play.

Debriefing

Begin the debriefing discussion with this question:

- *If you were a Rule Sheet Referee, what interesting things did you observe?*

Conduct the remainder of the debriefing discussion by asking questions such as:

- *How many of you won the game? How do you feel about it?*
- *How many of you lost the game? How do you feel about it?*
- *How many of you have not completed the game? How do you feel about it?*
- *How many of you used the strategy of both of you touching the Rule Sheet at the same time? How do you feel about it? How do the other players feel about this strategy?*
- *What are some of the different strategies that you have tried? How did they work?*
- *How many of assumed that if you win, the other player has to lose? What made you come up with this assumption?*
- *Did you think of win-win strategies? If you did not, what stopped you from doing so?*
- *What are different strategies that would have enabled both players to win?*
- *How would your behavior have changed if the winner received a cash prize?*
- *How would your behavior have changed, if there was a time limit of 30 seconds?*
- *How does the game reflect events in your workplace?*
- *How would you behave differently if we played the game again?*
- *Knowing what you learned from this activity, how would you change some of your behaviors in the workplace?*

Learning Points

1. Activities that involve winning automatically encourage competitive behavior.
2. If we are willing to think cooperatively, it is possible for everyone to win.

Follow-Up

You can add Jolt 27, Newton, immediately after this one because it incorporates similar learning points. You don't need to point out the similarities.

You WIN if you get the other person's right index finger to touch the Rule Sheet first.

You LOSE if your right index finger touches the Rule Sheet first.

Jolt 16
Free!

In his book, *Predictably Irrational*, Dan Ariely reports on experiments in which a significant majority of participants opted for a free gift certificate—even though the participants would have made a bigger profit by choosing a different option. Ariely's point is that the word FREE is so powerful that it frequently makes people behave in an irrational (and predictable) fashion. As he explains in his book, the difference between two cents and one cent is small. But the perceived difference between the two is huge.

 ## Synopsis

The facilitator distributes a contest entry form handout that offers participants a choice between two prize options in the form of gift cards. One of the choices is a $10 gift card that is awarded absolutely free, while the other choice is a $25 gift card that requires the winner to pay a $10 fee. The choices made by the participants allow the facilitator to lead a discussion about the power of FREE and how FREE sometimes causes us to make irrational choices.

 ## Purpose

- To experience how free offers distort our thinking

 ## Training Topic

- Critical thinking

 ## Participants

- One or more
- A larger participant pool is preferable because it ensures a more credible impact

 ## Time

- 2 minutes for the activity
- 5 to 10 minutes for the debriefing

Supplies

- Two gift cards, one for $10 and the other for $25

Handout

- One copy for each participant of Win a Fabulous Prize!

Caution

Make sure participants understand that only one winner will be selected and that the random selection process is open and fair.

Preparation

Buy the two gift cards ($10 and $25) before you conduct your session.

Flow

Distribute the handout. Give one copy of Win a Fabulous Prize! to each participant.

Give instructions. Ask the participants to read the handout and indicate on the handout their choice between the two fabulous prizes. Explain that you will randomly select *one winner* from the completed handouts. The person who filled out that handout will receive the prize he or she has selected.

Collect the choices. Give participants a minute or so to complete the handouts and set these completed handouts aside.

Check the data. Tell the group that you don't intend to waste their time by analyzing the data from the handouts. Instead, ask participants to raise their hands if they opted for the FREE alternative. You might make a joke by pointing out that this quick check of the data may be unreliable because some participants may be too embarrassed to confess making such an irrational choice.

Award the prize. Proceed by randomly picking a completed handout from the stack you set aside in order to award the promised prize. Give the participant who completed the handout you chose the appropriate gift card depending on the choice made.

Debriefing

Ask questions to help the participants figure out that those who selected the option of paying $10 made the better choice and would make a profit of $15.

Ask several participants why they selected the less profitable alternative.

Reassure these participants that they are not the only irrational people in the room by sharing the results of Dan Ariely's experiments.

Learning Points

1. It's a good practice to think before you rush to grab any FREE offer.
2. Always calculate the real cost and real benefits of every alternative you are given.

 Field Notes

Choose the gift cards carefully. Not every participant can use every gift card. Avoid special gift cards like those from a local or regional store. You might use gift cards from local malls if this is appropriate for your audience. We use American Express gift cards since redemption is easy.

Win a Fabulous Prize!

At the end of this session, I will randomly pick one completed handout. The person who filled out the handout will win a prize of his or her own choice.

Please write your name here: _____ .

Please select **one** of these two gift certificates as your prize. (*Note:* one prize is FREE, while the other prize costs some money.)

☐ $10 Gift Card for FREE!
☐ $25 Gift Card for $10.00

Jolt 17
Free Time

This jolt makes its point by giving secret instructions to one group of participants while excluding a second group from any knowledge of these cultural clues. Thiagi has used this activity successfully in the middle of a diversity presentation with hundreds of participants assembled in an auditorium.

 ## Synopsis

Participants receive either a red or green dot as they enter the room. The red and green dots are used to separate the participants into two groups so that the facilitator can share secret information with one group and not the other to make a learning point about diversity and inclusion.

 ## Purpose

- To explore how it feels to be excluded—and to be the one excluding

 ## Training Topics

- Diversity
- Inclusion

 ## Participants

- Four or more
- Best group size is twenty to fifty

 ## Time

- 5 minutes for the activity
- 3 to 10 minutes for debriefing

Supplies

- A supply of green and red sticky dots
- A whistle
- A timer

Facilitator's Note

A set of slides (FreeTime.ppt) used to display secret instructions is included on the website for this book at www.pfeiffer.com/go/jolts (password: professional).

Caution

This jolt requires the facilitator to secretly compel one group of participants to ignore members of another group. Be ready to explain this stratagem (and to provide your rationale) during debriefing.

Preparation

Make sure that you have saved the FreeTime.ppt file to your laptop computer or flash drive for use in this activity.

Flow

Organize groups. As participants come to the session, randomly give each person a green dot or a red dot. Distribute approximately equal numbers of each color. Ask participants to stick the dots to their nametags or their forehead or any other highly visible spot.

Brief participants. In the middle of a presentation, ask all the participants to think of how they would like to spend 3 minutes of free time that you will shortly give them.

Assign planning strategies. Explain that you are going to conduct an experiment on right-brain and left-brain strategies for planning. Ask the participants to note the colored dot they were given as they walked into the room. Tell the participants with green dots to prepare a linear to-do list for the 3-minute period on any available piece of paper. Next, ask the participants who received red dots to close their eyes and just visualize what they will be doing during their 3 minutes of free time. Emphasize to the participants with red dots the importance of keeping their eyes closed until you blow your whistle.

Give secret instructions to greens. Begin projecting the set of seven slides on the screen, one at a time. The slides read:

- *Shhh! Follow these secrets instructions.*
- *When I blow the whistle, start an enthusiastic conversation. Share your ideas for how to spend the free 3-minute time period.*
- *But talk only to other greens. Ignore reds. Don't talk to them.*

- *Shout across chairs to other greens. If necessary, walk over to meet other greens.*
- *If reds talk to you, don't respond. Ignore them.*

Begin the free-time period. Turn off the projector. After about 1 minute blow your whistle and ask the participants with the red dots to open their eyes. Start the timer and invite all participants to discuss their plans for the remaining 2 minutes of free time. Watch the activities of the participants and how they interact with each other. Blow your whistle after 2 minutes and announce the end of the free-time period.

Debriefing

Conduct a debriefing discussion. Follow this suggested sequence for discussion:

- **Ask "How did you feel?"** Establish that the participants with the red dots felt uncomfortable about being ignored and excluded. Also establish that the participants with the green dots felt uncomfortable about ignoring and excluding other participants.
- **Ask "What happened?"** Ask participants for their explanations of what happened during the activity and why. The participants with green dots will likely explain that were merely following the instructions to ignore the others. Display the secret instructions on the screen again and continue with the debriefing.
- **Ask greens "Why?"** Discuss why the greens chose to follow the instructions to ignore the reds despite feeling uncomfortable. Point out that you indoctrinated these participants to follow this uncharacteristic behavior *in just a few seconds* and to imagine how strong their behavior might be if they had been acculturated to follow this behavior pattern for several years.
- **Relate to the workplace.** Ask the question, "In what ways is this activity similar to the dynamics in your own workplace?" Discuss the responses from your participants.
- **Ask "What if?" questions.** Use questions such as, "What if there were a higher number of reds than greens?" and "What if the free time period lasted for 10 minutes?"
- **Ask "What next?" questions.** Use questions such as, "Considering what you learned from this activity, how would you change the way you include or exclude people who belong to different groups in your organization?"

Learning Points

1. Participants felt uncomfortable during the exercise whether they were the victims of exclusion or the participants imposing the exclusionary behavior.
2. It is easy for people in a position of authority to set up norms of group behavior.

Variation

Do you feel uncomfortable about tricking people? Avoid using the jolt. Read the section on How to Benefit from a Jolt Without Conducting It in Chapter 4 for an alternative approach for presenting the learning point.

Jolt 18
How Fast?

Do you enjoy solving crossword puzzles or are you intimidated by them? Here's a jolt that incorporates a crossword puzzle to highlight how our self-images are partly based on comparison with others.

 ## Synopsis

Participants are asked to race against time to solve a crossword puzzle. What the participants don't realize is that there are two sets of clues for the same puzzle. Some players must struggle with difficult clues, while the others breeze through a much more easily solvable puzzle.

 ## Training Topics

- Problem solving
- Self-image

 ## Purpose

- To explore and discuss the impact on our self-esteem when we compare our performance with the performance of others

 ## Participants

- Two or more
- The best game involves ten to thirty players

 ## Time

- 5 minutes for the activity
- 5 to 10 minutes for debriefing

Supplies

- Pens or pencils
- Countdown timer
- Whistle

Handouts

- Two different versions of the same crossword puzzle prepared by the facilitator

Caution

Be careful not to reveal that there are two different versions of the crossword puzzle. To prevent this from happening, bring a single stack of alternating puzzles rather than distributing the puzzles from two separate stacks.

Preparation

Make copies of the crossword puzzle using the reproducible masters at the end of this jolt. The first two pages contain the easy clues and the next two contain the difficult clues. Make equal number of copies of both versions. Arrange a stack of handouts by alternating the two versions.

Flow

Distribute crossword puzzles. Give each participant a copy of the puzzle. (It does not matter who receives the easy version and who receives the difficult version.) Set your countdown timer for 4 minutes and ask participants to solve the puzzle as quickly as possible. Tell the players to stand up when they have solved the entire puzzle.

Recognize fast solvers. When a player stands up to indicate that the puzzle has been solved, announce the completion time and congratulate the player.

Stop the activity. At the end of 4 minutes, blow your whistle and ask everyone to stop solving the puzzle. Congratulate the players who are standing up and ask them to sit down.

Read the solution. Ask everyone to check his or her answers as you read them. Read these answers (without reading any clues):

1 across: cat
2 across: ship
5 across: three
6 across: bed
7 across: ball
8 across: run

9 across: house
11 across: green
12 across: year
1 down: cash
3 down: hamburger
4 down: meeting
5 down: tea
7 down: book
10 down: sky

Compute scores. Point out that there are fifteen words in the puzzle and a perfect score will be 15 points (one point per word). Ask players to count the number of correct words and write down the score.

Debriefing

Begin a debriefing discussion. Invite players to discuss these questions:

- *How do you think the players who solved the entire puzzle (or most of the puzzle) feel about their performance?*

- *How do you think the players who solved only a small part of the puzzle feel about their performance?*

- *What is the impact of players' performance on their self-image?*

- *What is the impact of other players' performance on individual participants' self-images?*

Reveal the secret about two versions of clues. Explain that some players received a difficult set of clues, while others received an easy set. Choose a few players who used the hard version and a few who received the easy version and ask them to read the different versions of the word clues out loud.

Continue the debriefing. Ask questions similar to these:

- *How do you think the players who solved the entire puzzle (or most of the puzzle) feel about their performance after learning about the two sets of clues?*

- *How do you think the players who solved only a small part of the puzzle feel about their performance after learning about the two sets of clues?*

- *How did the knowledge of the two sets of clues affect your self-image?*

- *How does the activity reflect events in your workplace?*

- *Does your self-image suffer damage in the workplace just because you were slower than your co-workers?*

- *What is the workplace equivalent of receiving easy and difficult clues?*

- *What would have happened if only one player received the difficult set of clues and everyone else finished solving the puzzles?*

Summarize major insights from the debriefing discussions. Ask players how they would apply their new insights to their workplace performance.

Learning Points

1. Our self-image is influenced by comparing our performance with the performances of others.
2. Similar tasks may have hidden factors that increase or decrease the difficulty for some people.

 ## Variations

Are you working with non-English speakers? Instead of a crossword puzzle, use a Sudoku puzzle. Use more or fewer numbers in the initial set to modify the difficulty level of the puzzle.

Would you like to speed up the activity? Stop the puzzle-solving part after 2 minutes. Read the answers and have participants score their performance.

 ## Field Notes

Most people in our workshops are able to solve the **easy** puzzle in less than 3 minutes.

How Fast? Puzzle

Across

1. An animal that says "Meow"

2. Ocean liner (big boat)

5. Two plus one

6. What do you sleep on?

7. A round object that is used in different games

8. Moving faster than when you walk

9. Building in which you live

11. Color of grass

12. 12 months make up a _____.

Down

1. What do you get from an ATM machine?

3. Popular fast-food item in the U.S.

4. Coming together to discuss things

5. Coffee, _____, or milk?

7. Bound copy of printed pages. You can order one from *Amazon.com*.

10. Blue region about the earth

How Fast? Puzzle

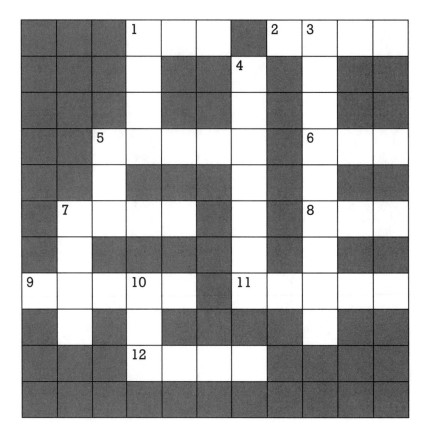

Across
1. Feline mammal
2. Transport commercially
5. A prime number that is greater by a unit than two
6. The ground under a body of water
7. A pitch that is not in the strike zone
8. An unbroken series of events
9. Aristocratic family line
11. naïve and easily deceived
12. Time taken by a planet in the solar system to make a complete revolution around the sun

Down
1. Money in the form of bills or coins
3. Resident of a port city in Germany
4. Coming together for business, social, or religious purposes
5. An eastern Asian evergreen shrub having fragrant glossy leaves that are dried to prepare a hot beverage.
7. To arrange for tickets in advance
10. The celestial region

Jolt 19
How Many Squares?

We are frequently complacent and accept the most obvious answers when solving problems. This jolt emphasizes the need to re-examine our initial conclusions and to think more deeply. Participants are admonished to take a second look at their initial conclusions and to discover more accurate solutions.

 ## Synopsis

Participants are asked to count the number of squares in a series of projected grids. The grids are constructed in such a way that makes it difficult for the participants to count them correctly. At the end of the activity, the facilitator leads the participants through a process that demonstrates the correct way to count the grids and arrive at the right answer.

 ## Purpose

- To examine our tendency to impulsively answer questions or solve problems instead of using a systematic, thoughtful, and more accurate process

 ## Training Topics

- Mindfulness
- Critical thinking
- Problem solving

 ## Participants

- One or more

 ## Time

- 2 minutes for the activity
- 3 to 7 minutes for debriefing

Facilitator's Note

Thirty-eight PowerPoint slides (Squares.ppt) are found on the website for this book at www.pfeiffer.com/go/jolts (password: professional).

 ## Equipment

- LCD projector
- Screen

 ## Preparation

Install the slide file in your laptop computer or zip drive. Connect your computer or zip drive to an LCD projector and make sure the slides can be projected.

 ## Flow

Pose the question. Project Slide 1 with the question, "How many squares do you see in this figure?" Immediately advance to the next slide (Slide 2) that shows a 5-by-5 grid. Tell the participants that they have 45 seconds to count the total number of squares in the projected image and announce the beginning of the activity.

Collect the responses. After 45 seconds, announce the end of the activity. Ask participants to call out the total number of squares. It is likely that you hear different responses, ranging from 25 to 60. Repeat several of the different responses and emphasize that they range widely. Act surprised and say that you are going to count the squares. Ask the participants to help you in the process.

Count the squares. Project the next two slides (Slides 3 and 4) and gain agreement on the fact that there are 25 squares that are 1 by 1 in size.

Move on to the next set of slides (Slides 5 to 20). Project Slide 5 (*There are 16 2-by-2 squares*) and proceed one slide at a time to show the participants that the grid indeed contains 16 squares that are 2 by 2 in size.

Proceed to the next set of slides (Slides 21 to 30). Project slide 21 (*There are 9 3-by-3 squares*) and proceed one slide at a time to show participants that the grid contains 9 squares, 3 by 3 in size.

Show the next set of slides (Slides 31 to 35). Project Slide 31 (*There are 4 4-by-4 squares*) and proceed one slide at a time to show participants that the grid contains four squares, 4 by 4 in size.

Display the next two slides (Slides 36 and 37). Project Slide 36 (*There is 1 5-by-5 square*) and proceed to display Slide 37 to show that the grid contains a single 5-by-5 square.

Move to the last slide (Slide 38). Project slide 38 that provides an overview of all the squares you have counted. Make sure everyone agrees there are fifty-five total squares in the figure.

Congratulate people who counted the correct number of squares. Identify the participants who came up with the correct answer—or the closest number of to the correct answer. Lead a round of applause.

Debriefing

Conduct a debriefing discussion with these questions:

- *How confident do you feel that fifty-five is the correct answer?*
- *How confident did you feel about your earlier answer if it was different from fifty-five?*
- *If you gave the correct answer earlier, how did you arrive at it? Was it because you have seen this problem before and remembered the answer?*
- *Encourage participants to come up with real-world examples of jumping to conclusions only to find out later that an answer was not correct.*

Learning Points

1. Some participants are confident even though they have the wrong answer.
2. Logical and systematic approaches are better strategies for arriving at accurate and credible answers than jumping to intuitive conclusions.
3. It is useful to re-examine all answers.

Variations

Takes too long to show different squares? Here's a faster jolt: Use a 3-by-3 grid and ask the same question. The total number of squares in this figure is fourteen (9 squares, 1 by 1 in size; 4 squares, 2 by 2 in size; and 1 square, 3 by 3 in size).

Don't have access to computers, PowerPoint slides, and an LCD projector? Use a flip chart. Draw a 5-by-5 grid. It helps if your flip-chart paper has light squares. Use cardboard cutouts of 1-by-1, 2-by-2, 3-by-3, 4-by-4, and 5-by-5 squares. Move the cutout on the flip-chart grid to show and count squares of different sizes.

Jolt 20
Last Week

The past affects our present happiness. Instead of brooding or ruminating over bitter, hostile, and resentful experiences, we can increase our happiness by savoring the past with gratitude, pride, and contentment. This jolt demonstrates how our current emotions are determined by the nature of our thoughts about the past.

Synopsis

In this jolt, participants work with two different versions of the same questionnaire. One version focuses on the problems of the previous week, while the other focuses on events that elicit feelings of gratitude. The debriefing that follows examines the impact of positive and negative thinking on present happiness.

Purpose

- To explore how rumination about past problems or disappointments impacts current happiness as well as the alternate choice of savoring the past

Training Topics

- Happiness
- Motivation
- Gratitude

Participants

- One or more

Time

- 3 minutes for the activity
- 5 to 10 minutes for debriefing

Handouts

- Two versions of the Last Week Questionnaire, one version for half the participants and one for the other half

Caution

Be careful not to reveal that there are two different versions of the questionnaire. Use a single stack of questionnaires containing both versions rather than distributing the handouts from two separate stacks.

Preparation

Make copies of both versions of the handout. Make approximately one-half of the problem oriented and one-half gratitude oriented.

Flow

Distribute the questionnaire. Give one copy of the questionnaire (from the combined stack) to each participant. (Everyone will assume they have the same questionnaire.)

Give instructions. Ask participants to take a few minutes to respond to the questionnaire. Emphasize that the answers are for "their eyes only" and that nobody will be required to share responses. Tell participants that they can write short cryptic responses only they understand.

Check on the emotional response. After making sure that everyone has completed the questionnaire, ask participants whether the act of responding to the questionnaire changed their mood to a more positive or a more negative state than before. Ask the participants who began feeling more positive during the activity to stand up and tell those who had a more negative response to remain seated.

Check the impact of the questionnaire. Reveal the secret that two versions of the questionnaire were handed out. Read a question from the rumination version followed by a question from the gratitude version and point out the difference. Ask participants who received the gratitude questionnaire to raise their hands (while continuing to be standing or sitting).

Debriefing

Debrief participants. More of the people who are standing will likely raise their hands (compared to those sitting down). Conduct a discussion that emphasizes how emotions are impacted by thinking about past difficulties. Ask the participants to supply real-world examples of this principle and brainstorm strategies for increasing grateful thoughts about the past.

Learning Points

1. Our current perceptions are affected by how we feel about the past.
2. Gratitude about the past increases our current happiness.
3. Focusing on past problems make us more unhappy in the present.
4. We can increase our happiness by savoring positive memories and by not ruminating on negative memories.

Variation

Don't want to use questionnaires? Divide your group into an even number of teams. Give two different versions of cards you have prepared ahead of time with different discussion topics for each team. Give half of the teams the topic of events that made the participants happy. Give the other half discussion topics about problems faced the previous week. Give the teams 4 minutes to discuss their respective topics.

Last Week Questionnaire

Instructions: Think back on what happened last week. Recall three problems you faced that frustrated you and made you feel unhappy.

List these events briefly below.

You do not have to share your response with anyone else. So you can write them down in an abbreviated or cryptic fashion.

1. _____

_____

_____

_____

_____

2. _____

_____

_____

_____

_____

3. _____

_____

_____

_____

_____

Last Week Questionnaire

Instructions: Think back on what happened last week. Recall three events that made you feel grateful.

List these events briefly below.

You do not have to share your response with anyone else. So you can write them down in an abbreviated or cryptic fashion.

1. _____

   _____

   _____

   _____

   _____

2. _____

   _____

   _____

   _____

   _____

3. _____

   _____

   _____

   _____

   _____

Jolt 21
Limits

With all the electronic devices around, it's not uncommon to have a participant who is alternatively listening to you, texting friends, and searching for something on Google. Some people are confident that multitasking allows them to accomplish more. Others believe that multitasking has limitations and might actually slow us down. Here's an amusing jolt that lets your participants discover how difficult it can be to combine just two simple activities.

 ## Synopsis

Participants are asked to draw an imaginary number in the air with their right index fingers while at the same time drawing a circle in a clockwise direction with their left feet. This activity results in hilarious behavior but offers some powerful lessons for the participants.

 ## Purpose

- To examine how multitasking may actually waste time and reduce accuracy

 ## Training Topics

- Multitasking
- Time management

 ## Participants

- One or more

 ## Time

- 2 minutes for the activity
- 3 to 7 minutes for debriefing

 ## Caution

This activity requires certain amount of coordination and balance. Make sure that overenthusiastic participants don't fall down.

Flow

Demonstrate the right-hand activity. Give these instructions (in your own words), demonstrating each step.

- *Please stand up.*
- *Raise your right hand and extend your index finger.*
- *Write a large number 6 in the air.*
- *Lower your hand.*

Demonstrate the right-foot activity. Give these instructions (in your own words), demonstrating each step:

- *Lift your right foot a few inches above the ground.*
- *Draw a large circle in a clockwise direction with your foot.*
- *Keep drawing large clockwise circles.*

Give instructions for the multitasking activity. Give these instructions (in your own words). You don't have to demonstrate the steps:

- *Continue drawing large clockwise circles with your foot.*
- *Now combine this with the first activity.*
- *Write a large number 6 with your finger.*
- *Make sure that you are drawing clockwise circles with your foot at the same time.*

 Debriefing

Explain to the participants that they performed a multitasking activity and point out that most people find it impossible or very difficult to do this multitasking.

Ask the participants what they learned from the activity. Keep probing to elicit this learning point: *Be careful about doing more than one thing at a time. You may end up performing both tasks poorly.*

Point out that some combinations of activities lend themselves more to efficient multi-tasking than others and invite the participants to share examples of these two types.

 Learning Points

1. Multitasking does not necessarily result in greater efficiency.
2. It may be impossible to perform some tasks in combination.
3. Multitasking may invite errors and actually slow down progress.

Variation

Do you need a less hazardous activity? Try the children's activity of rubbing your tummy in a circular motion with one hand while tapping your head with the other hand.

Jolt 22
Long Words

Magicians sometimes use an accomplice in the audience to help them perform intriguing or astounding tricks. Long Words is not a magic trick, but it uses an accomplice to drive home an important learning point about long-term planning.

 ## Synopsis

Participants must use the twenty letters provided in a handout to create three words during three rounds of play. A secretly trained accomplice wins, and the facilitator uses the trick to drive home the learning point about planning.

 ## Purpose

- To emphasize the importance of long-term planning

 ## Training Topic

- Planning

 ## Participants

- Two or more
- The best game involves ten to twenty participants

 ## Time

- 5 minutes for the activity
- 5 to 15 minutes for debriefing

 ## Supplies

- Pencils
- A whistle

Handout

- One copy of Long Words Handout for each participant

Preparation

Before conducting the game, find a suitable secret accomplice. Explain that you are going to play a word game in three rounds. Provide a copy of the handout to the secret participant and ask him or her to read it. Make sure that the participant understands how to play the game and explain that you will teach him or her a secret strategy that will guarantee a victory in the game. Ask the participant to memorize these three words and use them in this order for the three rounds of the game:

I

MANAGEMENT

REPORTERS

Explain to your accomplice that he or she will lose the first round but will likely win the next two rounds.

Flow

Distribute copies of the handout. Ask the participants to read the instructions.

Conduct the first round. Blow your whistle to signal the start of the first round, count for 30 seconds and then blow your whistle again to conclude the round. Ask the participants to show their words to each other. Declare the player with the longest word as the winner for the first round. You may have a tie for the first round, but make sure your accomplice loses this round.

Conduct the second round. Repeat the contest procedure. Your accomplice will win this round—unless some other player has figured out a similar strategy.

Conduct the third round. Repeat the contest procedure one more time. Your accomplice will win this round as well.

Identify the game winner. Congratulate your accomplice for having won the most rounds.

Debriefing

Confess to the participants that you had shared the winning strategy with an accomplice before the game started. If any of the other participants came up with a similar strategy, congratulate them for their strategic thinking. Ask participants to think back on the experience and to analyze the winning strategy. Ask appropriate questions to elicit these learning points:

Learning Points

1. It is important to come up with proactive plans for long-term results.
2. Time limits tempt us to ignore proactive planning.

3. Most of us don't have the patience to reflect on future implications of current behavior.
4. You may win the battle, but lose the war. Participants who win the first round are likely to lose the ensuing two rounds.

 Field Notes

In case you are curious, here are some of the words that our sophisticated participants have come up with during the first round of play in our classes:

> agreements, anteaters, apartments, arraignments, arrangements, enterprise, entertainers, estrangement, generators, impersonate, interpreter, interrogate, magistrate, mainstream, pragmatism, prearrangement, presentations, presentiment, programmers, protesting, rearrangements, regenerate, regeneration, remonstrate, renegotiates, representation, retirement, ringmaster, segmentation, stagnation, tangerines, transparent, and transporting

Long Words Handout

A, A, E, E, E, E, G, I, M, M, N, N, O, P, R, R, R, S, T, T

Instructions: Study the twenty letters above. Some letters (A, E, M, N, R, and T) are repeated more than once and some letters (B, C, D, F, H, J, K, L, Q, U, V, W, X, Y, and Z) are missing.

You (and all other players) have the same twenty letters.

This game is played in three rounds. You win each round of the game if you create the longest word *using as many of these letters as possible*. The letters that you use during each round will not be available for the subsequent rounds.

Round 1

When you hear the whistle, begin making up words. You have 30 seconds to come up with an English word using any of the letters above.

Write your word here: _____

Stop when you hear the whistle.

Cross out the letters used for making your word. You should not use these letters in future rounds of the game.

Round 2

When you hear the whistle again, start the second round.

Write your word here: _____.

Stop when you hear the whistle again. Cross out the letters used for making your word. Do not use any of the crossed-out letters in the next round.

Round 3

Let's play another round of the game as before.

Write your word here: _____

Jolt 23
Me and My Team

As a member of a team, you frequently face conflicts between your personal needs and the needs of the team. This jolt focuses on these conflicts.

 ## Synopsis

This jolt requires the members of a team to allocate limited resources between themselves and the other team members. The choices that each team member makes in how he wishes to allocate limited resources can mean the difference between winning personally and winning as a team.

 ## Purpose

- To explore how self-interest and the common interest of a team are often in conflict

 ## Training Topics

- Trust
- Teamwork

 ## Participants

- Eight or more
- The best number of participants is fifteen to thirty

 ## Time

- 3 minutes for the activity
- 7 to 15 minutes for debriefing

 ## Supplies

- Index cards
- Pens or pencils

137

- Countdown timer
- Whistle

Caution

Team members may resent the winner of the game. Remind the participants that this is just a game and to not make a big issue out of a team member's decisions about point allocation.

Flow

Form teams. Divide the group into two or more teams, each with four to six members. Make sure that all teams have equal numbers of participants. If you have additional members, have them play the role of observers or auditors.

Brief the participants. Explain that each player has 100 resource points to distribute and that they may disseminate the points as they wish. Say that each player may keep all 100 points for personal use, donate all the points to the team, or do anything in between. Points donated to the team belong to the team as a whole and not to any individual member.

Explain the formula for winning. *The winner is the player with the highest personal score as well as being a member of the team with highest team score.* Point out that if a team member keeps all the points for herself (in order to have the highest personal score), the team may lose the opportunity to have the highest team score.

Ask team members to record their decisions. Distribute blank index cards to all participants and ask each to write his or her name on the top. Next, ask participants to *secretly* write the number of resource points they want to keep for themselves. Then ask the participants to write the number of resource points they are willing to contribute to the team. Emphasize that these two numbers should add up to 100.

Compute team scores. After a suitable pause, ask participants to fold their index cards and give them to you (or to your auditor). Keep the cards that belong to each team separate from the others and compute the total team score for each team.

Identify the winner. Once the scores have been computed, announce the total points earned by each team. Identify the team with the highest team score, and read the name of the individual with the highest personal score. Congratulate this winner. (There may be more than one winner because of ties. In that case identify and congratulate all the winners.)

Debriefing

Ask and discuss the following types of questions:

- *How do you think the winner feels about his or her victory?*
- *How do you think the team members feel about the winner?*
- *How did you make the decision about distributing the resource points?*

- *What assumptions did you make about your teammates' decisions?*
- *Did your level of trust about your teammates go up or go down as a result of playing this game?*
- *How does this game reflect the events in your workplace?*
- *What would have happened if the facilitator did not reveal the name of the winner?*
- *What would have happened if the winner received a cash prize?*
- *What would have happened if team members were permitted to talk with each other before recording their point distributions? (The information on the index cards was kept secret.)*

Learning Points

1. Frequently, self-interest and team-interest clash.
2. Secrecy reduces trust in a team.

Variation

Do you want to maximize the learning from this game? Conduct two more rounds. During the second round, permit team members to strategize with each other before secretly distributing their resource points. During the third round, announce a cash prize for the winner.

Jolt 24
Memory Test

How do we remember what we remember? Here's a quick jolt that helps participants discover basic psychological facts about memory.

 Synopsis

Participants are given a short amount of time to review a list of words, then are asked to recall as many words as possible. The facilitator leads the participants through a series of questions that demonstrate four key principles of memory.

 Purpose

- To demonstrate the function of human memory and recall

 Caution

Calling this activity a "test" may make some participants anxious even after your assurance that the intent is to make a learning point. Be prepared for those participants who insist on getting it right.

 Training Topics

- Memory
- Communication

 Participants

- One or more

 Time

- 5 minutes for the jolt
- 5 to 10 minutes for debriefing

Supplies

- Pen or pencils
- Paper
- Timer

Facilitator's Note

A recorded version of the memory test is included on the website for this book at www.pfeiffer.com/go/jolts. You may use this instead of reading the test words.

Flow

Brief participants. Tell the participants that you will administer a memory test as part of this activity and that the test involves listening to and recalling a standardized list of words. Tell the participants to listen carefully to these words when you play (or say) them, but to not write any words down on paper. Say that a test will come later to see how many words each participant can recall.

Present words. Read the following list of words. Pause briefly between one word and the next. Do not change the sequence. One of the words (*night*) is used three times.

dream
sleep
night
mattress
snooze
sheet
nod
tired
night
artichoke
insomnia
blanket
night
alarm
nap
snore
pillow

Administer the recall test. Pause for about 10 seconds after you have completed reading the words or you have listened to the recording. Ask the participants to write as many of the words as they can remember on any available piece of paper. Wait for about 40 seconds to give the participants time to complete the task.

Explain your intent. Reassure participants that you are not interested in finding out how each person performed on the test. Instead, you will use the test to explore four basic principles about memory.

Debriefing

Explain each of the four important principles about memory, using data from the participants' performance on the test:

- **Primacy and recency effects.** Ask participants to raise their hands if they recalled the words *dream* and *pillow*. Explain that most people remember the first and the last things in a series of words. Most participants will likely have written *dream* and *pillow* because these were the first and the last words in the list.
- **Surprise effect.** Ask participants to raise their hands if they wrote down the word *artichoke*. Explain that people have a tendency to remember anything that is novel or different. You should find that most participants wrote down *artichoke* because it is different from the other words in the list.
- **Repetition effect.** Ask the participants to raise their hands if they recalled the word *night*. Explain that repetition is a key factor in recall. Since the word night is repeated three times, most participants will have this word on their recall lists.
- **False-memory effect.** Ask the participants to raise their hands if they recalled the word *bed*. A few people will likely raise their hands in response to this question. Explain that this word was not on your original list. Explain that the human brain has a tendency to close logical gaps in what we hear, see, or read, and frequently this effect provides us with memories of things or events that never took place.

Ask the participants how they might use these four principles to help them remember new terms and ideas in the training session they are currently attending. Give an example statement such as, "I will use the primacy and the recency effect to remember what is said in the middle of the training session by repeating the key ideas to myself several times."

Ask the participants how they might use these four principals to help their employees or customers remember key points. Give an example statement such as, "I will position the points or messages I want my customers or employees to remember at the beginning and end of my statements. I will also use the principle of repetition to spur the memory and recall of employees and customers."

 Learning Points

1. If you apply the four principals of memory, you increase your ability to recall.
2. You can use these simple principles to help your customers or employees remember important points and key information.

 Variation

Want to customize this jolt to relate more to your topic? Change the list of words. Make sure you repeat one of the words three times, and be sure to insert a novelty word somewhere in the middle to represent the surprise principle.

Jolt 25
Mingle

Working with people from different cultures means that we must be sensitive to different behavioral expectations. Rather than reading about how to deal with these differences, this jolt provides participants with a first hand experience that delivers an important cultural message.

 ## Synopsis

Participants in this jolt pretend they are attending a party and must follow the instructions on a secret *Etiquette Card* provided by the facilitator. Some of the behaviors the participants are instructed to do are unusual, contradictory, and confusing. A debriefing discussion that follows the "party" focuses on dealing with differences in cultural norms.

 ## Purpose

- To explore different rules of etiquette and cultural taboos

 ## Training Topics

- Diversity
- Inclusion

 ## Participants

- Five or more
- The best group size is fifteen to fifty

 ## Time

- 3 minutes for the activity
- 5 to 10 minutes for debriefing

Handout

- Etiquette cards on index stock (to be prepared using the Mingle Handout), one card for each participant.

Caution

Some participants may be uncomfortable behaving as the Etiquette Card instructs. However, most of the participants soon realize that everyone else is following the unusual demands and relax.

Preparation

Prepare etiquette cards from the list on the Mingle Handout and give one to each participant.

Start each card with this message:

This is your etiquette card. Please do not show it to anyone else. Read the message in secret and put away the card.

You may use the rules provided in the handout or create your own messages. You may also repeat the same message on more than one card if you anticipate a lot of participants.

Flow

Distribute etiquette cards. As the participants enter the training room, give each an Etiquette Card.

Join the party. Ask participants to pretend that they are at a party. Urge them to get together in small groups and discuss any topic of their choice.

Behave appropriately. Ask participants to behave courteously according to the rules on their Etiquette Cards during the conversation without revealing what this rule instructs them to do.

Conclude the party. After about 3 minutes, announce the end of the party, gather all the cards, and conduct a debriefing discussion.

Debriefing

Ask participants to point to the person who behaved in the most bizarre fashion. Point out the acceptable behaviors (and even preferred behaviors) in some of the groups as examples.

Use the same procedure to identify and discuss the most irritating behaviors, the most alien behaviors, and the most comical behaviors.

 ## Learning Points

1. Behaviors or customs that one person views as polite or acceptable may be rude or inappropriate to another person.
2. Everyone feels uncomfortable behaving outside his or her cultural norms.

 ## Variation

Want to change the context? Instead of staging a party, ask participants to pretend they are at a picnic or in a business meeting. The etiquette cards cover a wide variety of situations, so you can be creative.

Mingle Handout

It is impolite to stand aloof, so stand close to the others until you almost touch them. If someone backs off, keep moving closer.

It is impolite to crowd people, so maintain your distance. Stand away so that there is at least an arm's length between you and the nearest person. If anyone gets too close to you, back off until you have achieved the required distance.

It is impolite to shout, so talk softly. Whisper even when people cannot hear you; do not raise your voice.

It is impolite to talk to more than one person at the same time. Always talk to a single individual standing near you so that you can have a private conversation. Do not address your remarks to the group as a whole.

It is impolite to stare at people, so avoid eye contact. Look at the floor or the speaker's shoes. Do not look directly at the speaker's face.

It is important to get people's attention before you speak, so hold your hand above your head and snap your fingers. Do this every time you make a statement or ask a question. That's the polite way to get everyone's attention.

It is friendly to share your thoughts and feelings without any inhibition. So feel free to make self-disclosure statements. Describe your intimate feelings about different subjects. Ask personal questions of the other members of the group.

It is polite and reassuring to reach out and touch someone. Touch people on the arm or the shoulder when you speak to them.

It is important to show your enthusiasm. So jump in before other speakers have finished their sentences and add your ideas. Remember, it is rude to hold back your thoughts.

It is impolite to be blunt and tactless. It is preferable to talk in abstractions and to approach the subject in an indirect fashion.

It is impolite to speak impulsively. Whenever somebody asks you a question, silently count to seven before you give the answer.

Jolt 26
New Word

Sometimes smart people make dumb mistakes. Complacency is one cause. After all, even smart people have a tendency to resist shifting strategies, especially when that strategy is familiar and has a history of working. This jolt explores the need to sometimes shift strategies.

 ## Synopsis

Participants are asked to solve an initial puzzle that requires them to come up with a successful strategy to find a solution. When a second puzzle, very similar to the first, is introduced, the participants discover that the strategy used to solve the first puzzle is not appropriate for the new puzzle.

 ## Purpose

- To explore the need for flexible thinking

 ## Training Topics

- Problem solving
- Creative thinking

 ## Participants

- One or more

 ## Time

- 3 minutes for the activity
- 5 to 15 minutes for debriefing

Facilitator's Note

A set of nine PowerPoint slides can be found on the website for this book at www .pfeiffer.com/go/jolts.

Preparation

Copy the slides to your laptop computer or zip drive. Ensure that your LCD project is in working order and take a few minutes to flip through the slides thinking about the progression of images from the perspective of the participant.

 Equipment

- Laptop computer
- LCD projector
- Screen

 Flow

Brief the participants. Display the title slide. Explain that the activity involves solving a word puzzle.

Display the puzzle. Project the next three slides one after the other. Point out that the second slide contains two words.

NEW
DEER

Read the instruction from Slide 3:

- *Rearrange the seven letters from the two words to form one word.*

Display Slide 4 that shows the two words again.

Reveal the solution. Wait until one or more participants have solved the puzzle. (If necessary, give some hints to speed up the process.) Congratulate the successful participants. Display Slide 5 so everyone can see the solution:

RENEWED

Display the next puzzle. Display Slide 6 and explain that this is the next puzzle.

NEW
DOOR

Do not imply that this puzzle is of the same type as the previous one. Let the puzzle speak for itself.

Show Slide 7 and read the instruction below.

- *Rearrange the seven letters from the two words to form one word.*

Proceed to Slide 8 and invite participants to solve the puzzle.

Reveal the solution. If any participants have correctly solved the puzzle, congratulate them. Display Slide 9 with the solution. **You can count on a few good natured (we hope) but hostile shouts.**

ONE WORD

Debriefing

Conduct your debriefing discussion by asking questions such as:

- *Did you solve the New + Deer puzzle? How did you feel about it?*
- *Did you solve the New + Door puzzle? How did you feel about it?*
- *We used different strategies for solving the two different puzzles. What are the major differences?*
- *The way to solve the second puzzle is to follow the instructions literally. However, most people complicate the task by trying to find a creative solution that involves a single word. Why does this happen?*
- *What would have happened if we began with the second puzzle first and the presented you with the New + Deer puzzle?*

 Learning Points

1. The strategy for solving one problem may not work with another problem.
2. Problems that appear to be very similar may require significantly different strategies to solve.
3. Sometimes it is a good idea to think inside the box and literally follow given instructions.

 Field Notes

Do you have more time to spend? Here are more two-word combinations you can solve by the first type of strategy. (The solutions are given in parentheses.) You may want to use several of these combinations before ending up with the New + Door puzzle. This ensures participants are following a fixed pattern.

NEW + SOAP (weapons)
NEW + RODS (wonders or downers)
NEW + LIDS (swindle)
NEW + BEET (between)

Jolt 27
Newton

Newton's third law says that *for every action, there is an equal and opposite reaction.* This classic scientific maxim is illustrated by this jolt, even though it has nothing to do with physics.

 ## Synopsis

Pairs of participants face each other and engage in a mild physical power game to demonstrate a learning point about cooperative solutions.

 ## Purpose

- To explore negotiating win-win solutions

 ## Training Topics

- Negotiation
- Cooperation
- Competition

 ## Participants

- Two or more
- The best game involves ten to forty participants

 ## Time

- 2 minutes for the activity
- 5 to 15 minutes for debriefing

 ## Supplies

- Countdown timer
- Whistle

Flow

Give initial instructions. Ask the participants to pair up and stand facing each other. Ask them to plant their feet firmly on the ground. They should next raise both hands to an outstretched position in front of their bodies and place their hands palm to palm against their partners' hands.

Explain how to win. Say that the participant who forces his or her partner to move his or her feet within 17 seconds will win the activity. Repeat this rule a couple of times to ensure the participants understand.

Begin the activity. Blow your whistle and start the timer. Most participants will use brute force against each other in order to win the game. A few savvy martial-arts practitioners may suddenly stop pushing and let a partner's momentum do the work of making him or her topple forward.

Stop the activity. After 17 seconds, blow your whistle and stop the activity.

 Debriefing

Ask participants to think back on the experience and compare the different strategies used for winning.

Ask a volunteer to come forward for a quick strategy demonstration. Assume the initial face-to-face, palm-to-palm position. Blow the whistle and move your feet immediately. Tell the other person, "You've won! We still have 11 more seconds. Would you mind moving your feet so I can win also?"

After the demonstration, participants may complain that you cheated. Point out that the rule set out at the beginning merely required you to make the other person move his or her feet within 17 seconds. Point out that there was no prohibition against moving your own feet.

Continue with the debriefing, bringing out learning points related to making assumptions, creating win-win solutions, modeling appropriate behaviors, managing conflicts, and the futility of meeting force with force.

 Learning Points

1. *Winning* does not always require that someone *lose*.
2. A win-win solution to conflict is often preferable.
3. When participants stand face-to-face, confrontational approaches are encouraged.

 Variations

Does the physical nature of the activity feel uncomfortable? Use Jolt 15, First Touch, which employs a similar approach to drive home the same point, but without physical confrontation.

Do you have an odd number of participants? It is fine to pair up with the participant who is left out.

Jolt 28
Next Action

We are enthusiastic users of David Allen's time-management technique as described in his book, *Getting Things Done*. Here's a jolt that incorporates one of David Allen's powerful principles.

 ## Synopsis

In this jolt, participants are led through an activity that encourages action and problem solving. It explores how using a few simple techniques can impact our lives, attitudes, and outlooks in positive, powerful ways.

 ## Purpose

- To gain control and focus as a way to overcome troublesome situations

 ## Training Topics

- Time management
- Happiness

 ## Participants

- One or more

 ## Time

- 2 minutes for the activity
- 3 to 5 minutes for debriefing

 ## Supplies

- Paper and pencils

Flow

At a fairly rapid pace, give the participants these instructions to follow:

- *Write down a situation that bugs you and/or consumes an inordinate amount of your time. Describe this "in-your-face" situation in one or two sentences.*
- *Write down a single sentence that provides a specific successful outcome for this situation. In other words, what would need to happen for you to check the "Done" box next to this item?*
- *Write down the very next physical action required to move this situation forward. If you had nothing else to do in your life except to work for closure on this item, what visible action would you take?*

 Debriefing

Ask participants to raise their hands if they are experiencing at least a bit of enhanced control and increased happiness. Point out that the situation did not change but most people did acquire a clearer definition of the desired outcome and the next actions they might take. Remind the participants that all it took was a couple of minutes of action thinking to make them feel better.

 Learning Points

1. Too much thinking about troublesome situations is counterproductive.
2. A clear definition of a desired outcome focuses us on positive attention.
3. Small and tangible action steps move us in the right direction and reduce stress.

 Variation

Do you want to make this a collaborative activity? Ask a team of participants to go through the procedure by first selecting a common situation that bothers everyone on the team.

Jolt 29
Palm to Palm

We all have a tendency to reject, deny, or oppose ideas when we feel pressured to accept them. Here is a jolt that explores this built-in defense mechanism

 ## Synopsis

Participants use the automatic responses of bodies and minds to being pressured in order to make a point about better ways to deal with people.

 ## Purpose

- To demonstrate innate human characteristics about resistance to pressure

 ## Training Topics

- Communication
- Leadership
- Change management

 ## Participants

- One and more

 ## Time

- 2 minutes for the activity
- 3 to 5 minutes for the debriefing

Facilitator's Note

A recorded version of this jolt is included on the website for this book, www.pfeiffer .com/go/jolts. You may use this to give the instructions to the participants.

Flow

Give these instructions to the participants:

- *Please listen to these instructions and follow along.*
- *Place your hands in front of your chest, palm to palm.*
- *First, I am going to count to three. When I say "Three," I want you to push your right palm forcefully against your left palm.*
- *Are you ready? Here we go: One, two, three . . . push. . . .*
- *(Pause for 5 seconds.)*
- *Thanks. You may relax now.*

 Debriefing

Ask the participants whether their palms ended up on the left side of their body or remained in the middle of their bodies. (Most participants will say their palms remained in the middle.) Point out that if their palms remained in the middle it must mean that their left palms pushed back. Ask the participants why they think this happened when this outcome that was not a part of the instructions.

Explain to the participants that this activity is focused on what happened to their left palms and that you are not that interested in what happened with their right palms.

Probe the participants with additional questions and examples around this mysterious outcome to elicit the following learning points.

 Learning Points

1. People automatically resist when they feel they are being pushed.
2. This automatic reaction cuts across the entire range of human experience.

 Field Notes

If some participants in the room are familiar with this jolt, ask them to play along. This is important because participants may imitate others rather than follow directions. If too many participants do this, your learning points will not be as powerful or useful.

Jolt 30
Paper Money

This jolt is all about why we don't pay attention to details right in front of us.

Synopsis

Two players are paired and each player has an opportunity to answer questions about the details found on every $1 bill. The facilitator uses the players' lack of knowledge to make a point about the importance of paying attention to the details.

Purpose

- To slow down and notice the details associated with familiar objects

Training Topics

- Mindfulness
- Memory

Participants

- Two or more, divided into pairs

Time

- 3 minutes for the activity
- 3 to 5 minutes for debriefing

Supplies

- Ask the participants to each supply a $1 bill (or other common paper currency in your country). Note the suggestion below concerning players who do not have a $1 bill.

Flow

Pair up participants. Ask each participant to find a partner and sit (or stand) facing each other. If you end up with a single participant, it is fine for you to be the partner.

Show the money. Ask each pair of partners to produce a $1 bill. If any of the pairs cannot find a $1 bill, lend them one or ask them to borrow one from another player. Ask the partners to hold the single bill by its opposite corners so that each participant can see only one side of the bill.

Begin questioning. Ask the partner pairs to take turns asking questions about the side of the $1 bill they can see. Give some examples like the ones below:

- *How many times is the number 1 printed on my side?*
- *How many times is the word "one" spelled out on my side?*
- *How many digits does the serial number have?*
- *What three-dimensional shape is shown on my side?*
- *How many arrows does the eagle hold?*
- *Which direction is the eagle facing?*
- *Whose portrait is on the dollar bill?*

Explain the scoring system. Explain that the scoring system is based on immediate correct answers to questions about the $1 bill. Immediately after one partner asks a question about the $1 bill, the other partner must give an answer. A correct answer earns 1 point. An incorrect answer (or no answer) earns no points. After a suitable, short pause, the questioner must give the correct answer.

Switch sides. Stop the question-and-answer activity after 1 minute. Ask participants to turn the dollar bill around so they now see the side their partners used for questioning.

Continue questioning. Ask the partners to use the same procedure as before, asking and answering questions and keeping track of points. Conclude the round after 1 minute.

Debriefing

Conduct a quick debriefing. Ask participants to discuss how familiarity breeds "mindlessness." Ask what work-related supplies and tools are taken for granted? Talk about the dangers of ignoring familiar objects and people in organizations. Ask what could be gained by being mindful and paying attention to these objects and people.

Learning Points

1. We often don't pay attention to the details found in familiar objects.
2. In our workplaces, major trouble can be avoided by simply paying attention to the familiar people and variances from expected behavior.

Variation

How well do you know me? If you are facilitating a group of co-workers, you can invite members of each pair to take turns asking questions about each other. (For example, one participant might ask another: *Where did you work before you joined our organization?* or *Who is your favorite movie star?*)

Field Notes

Our apologies to international readers for using the dollar bill as the example. Obviously, you will be asking your players to use local currency. It's a good idea to carefully study both sides of the currency and memorize the details before you conduct the activity. After the debriefing, you might invite audience members to ask you questions about either side of the paper currency that you have chosen and impress them with your amazing knowledge.

Jolt 31
Photo Analysis

J udgment has many useful purposes. We use judgment to decide how to spend our time, who to do business with, and for other crucial decisions in our lives. Developing the ability to make judgments in a balanced way is important. However, too much of a judgmental approach may cause us to miss important opportunities and experiences. This jolt demonstrates how reducing our judging impulses can widen our frames of reference.

 ## Synopsis

Participants are shown a photograph projected on a screen and are asked to answer different versions of a questionnaire, one of which asks for a listing of *everything* they see and the other asking the participants to list only *interesting* things they see.

 ## Purpose

- To explore how judgment narrows our point of view

 ## Training Topic

- Mindfulness

 ## Participants

- Two or more

 ## Time

- 5 minutes for the activity
- 5 to 7 minutes for debriefing

Facilitator's Note

Use the slide for this activity (Photo Analysis.ppt) on the website www.pfeiffer.com/go/jolts or supply a photo slide of your own that shows a cluttered scene with a lot of elements (for example, a busy street scene or a crowded railway station).

Handouts

- Two different versions of the Photo Analysis handout

Equipment

- Laptop computer
- LCD projector
- Screen

Preparation

Copy the selected slide to your laptop computer or a zip drive. Make sure that the slide projects correctly. Prepare an equal number of copies of the two sets of instructions.

Caution

Be careful not to reveal that there are two different versions of the instructions. To prevent this from happening, bring a single stack of alternating instructions rather than distributing the handouts from two separate stacks.

Flow

Distribute handouts. Begin the session by randomly distributing a copy of the instructions to each participant.

Project the photo. Project the slide and make sure that the slide is in focus.

Tell participants that this is an independent activity. Ask the participants to read the instructions and record their responses on the handout. Wait for about 2 minutes for the participants to complete the work.

Total the responses. Ask the participants to count the total number of responses they wrote down and invite them to call out their totals. The results will fall into two groups; those who were asked to write down *everything* will have a significantly longer list than those who were asked to write down only the *interesting* things.

Debriefing

Debrief the activity by revealing the two different sets of instructions. Ask questions to emphasize the learning point that any type of judgment (such as looking for *interesting* things) reduces what you pay attention to a situation. Also point out that extreme judgments (such as *the most interesting*) will narrow the field significantly.

Jolts! Activities to Wake Up and Engage Your Participants

Encourage participants to keep an open mind in new situations to ensure they see all aspects presented to them. Remind the participants that a mindful person observes the world without judgment and does not conclude that a situation is either *good* or *bad*.

 Learning Points

1. Judging impacts our ability to be mindful.
2. Being judgmental affects our ability to make good decisions.
3. Being mindful means you keep an open mind in new situations.

Photo Analysis Handout

Instructions: Study the photograph carefully and write down as many of the things you see as possible.

_____

_____

_____

_____

_____

_____

_____

_____

_____

_____

_____

_____

_____

_____

_____

_____

_____

_____

_____

_____

_____

_____

_____

1

Photo Analysis Handout

Instructions: Study the photograph carefully and write down the interesting things that you see.

_____

_____

_____

_____

_____

_____

_____

_____

_____

_____

_____

_____

_____

_____

_____

_____

_____

_____

_____

_____

_____

_____

_____

_____

_____

2

Jolt 32
Positive Spin

This is our favorite closing activity because it helps us to conclude sessions on an upbeat note. It also presents an interesting learning point about interpreting the behavior of other people.

 ## Synopsis

Participants are asked to perform various activities and the facilitator demonstrates how it is possible to put a positive spin on almost anything.

 ## Purposes

- To bring the session to an upbeat and playful close
- To explore how we interpret the meaning of different activities

 ## Training Topics

- Playfulness
- Happiness

 ## Participants

- One or more
- This activity works best with ten to one hundred participants

 ## Time

- 2 minutes for the activity
- 2 minutes for debriefing

Flow

Show and tell. Give the following instructions. Demonstrate the appropriate action as you give each instruction.

- *Please stand up.*
- *Close your eyes. Keep them closed tightly.*
- *Now open your eyes. Make sure your eyes are open for the rest of the activity.*
- *Turn around completely so that you end up facing the same direction in which you started.*
- *Raise your right hand and make a fist. Bring it down and touch the left side of your chest three times.*
- *Please lower your hands.*

 Debriefing

Keep a poker face during the debriefing. Explain the meaning of the activity in a serious tone using a variation of this script:

- *Later, if anybody asks you about today's session, you can truthfully say:*
  - *It brought me to my feet.*
  - *It opened my eyes.*
  - *It turned me around completely.*
  - *It touched my heart.*

Ask the participants what they learned from the activity. Tell them what you learned from the activity. You might say:

- *It is not the activity, but the meaning we attach to it, that makes it important.*

End the session by wishing the participants the ability to put a positive spin on their own actions and the actions of other people.

 Learning Points

1. We can put a positive spin on everything we see and everything we do.
2. We become more positive ourselves when we interpret the events and the actions of other people in a positive way.

 Field Notes

We experimented with other activities (for example, pointing to the ceiling and interpreting it as "reaching to the sky"), but the four suggestions in the activity seem to be the best all-purpose ones. Experiment with other activities if you want, but don't clutter up this jolt too much.

Conducting an extended debriefing after this activity can be anticlimactic so it is best to just conclude with this activity and send your participants on their way.

Jolt 33
Psychic Cards

A quick magic trick with playing cards forms the basis of this jolt. Unlike secretive magicians, you reveal the trick to drive home an important learning point.

 ## Synopsis

The facilitator performs a card trick with the help of the participants in order to make an important learning point on mindfulness and focus.

 ## Purpose

- How an excessive focus on a single goal, process, or truth may lead to negative consequences

 ## Training Topics

- Mindfulness
- Goal focus

 ## Participants

- One or more

 ## Time

- 3 minutes for the jolt
- 5 to 15 minutes for the debriefing

Facilitator's Note

This jolt uses a set of PowerPoint slides (Psychic Cards.ppt) found at www.pfeiffer.com/go/jolts.

Equipment

- Laptop computer
- LCD projector
- Screen

 Preparation

Copy the slides to your laptop computer or zip drive. Connect to the LCD projector and make sure the images display correctly. Flip through the slides to experience the magic trick from the point of view of the participants.

 Flow

Brief the participants. Project the first three slides. Explain that this activity involves mind reading. Read the instructions from the slides.

Project the slide with the six playing cards. Project Slide 4 and remind participants to secretly select one of the six cards and remember it.

Explain the next part of the trick. Display Slides 5 through 7 and read the steps and instructions from the slides.

Display the slide with six cards. Show Slide 8. Note to the participants that one of these cards is face down. The participants will think the hidden card is their card (unless they know how the trick is done).

Here's how the trick is done. This explanation is for the facilitator only. Hold off on explaining the trick to the participants. The cards displayed in Slide 8 look very similar to the cards you displayed on Slide 4. However, none of these cards is the same. When the participants see the face-down card, they assume that the hidden card is the one they selected at the beginning of the activity. (Sorry for the anticlimax.)

Display the next two slides. Playfully claim that you are psychic and explain that the magic trick is actually a good example of the principles of perceptual psychology. Display Slides 9 and 10.

Explain the learning point. Display the next three slides (Slides 11 through 13). Explain that the cards in Slide 11 are the cards that you displayed at the beginning of the activity. Show Slide 12, which shows the cards that you displayed at the end of the activity. Show Slide 13 and point out that, even though the two sets of cards are very similar (in terms of numbers and suits), the cards are, in fact, not similar at all.

Let the participants figure out how the trick is done. Explain that we all tend to focus on what we perceive as most important. In this case, it was the card each participant chose. Once the choice was made, no other details about the other cards mattered. Because everyone was focused on successfully completing the task and engaged in finding just the card he or she had chosen, all other options and choices were ignored. Therefore, all the participants assumed the hidden card was their chosen card.

Display the final slide. Let the participants read the major learning point.

Debriefing

Invite participants to come up with real-world examples of an excessive focus on the details that result in our missing important tasks, experiences, or relationships. Here are some examples that participants are likely to suggest:

- *When you learn a new word, it keeps popping up in strange places.*
- *Excessive focus on a training objective prevents you from acquiring a broader understanding of the topic.*
- *Excessive focus on a single goal makes you ignore other opportunities.*
- *Infatuation with a person makes you overlook her faults.*
- *Unquestioning belief in a particular faith makes it difficult for fundamentalists to appreciate universal truths found in other religions.*
- *Enthusiastic belief in some new technique or methodology often results in illogical decision making.*

 Learning Point

1. Focusing on an element that is most important to you can lead to your missing other important elements in the situation.

 Field Notes

Don't worry about your inability to perform magic. If you use the set of slides provided, this trick will work automatically.

This magic trick is not exclusive to us and can be found easily on the Internet. As a result of its availability, some of your participants may have seen it done. At the beginning ask whether any of the participants are familiar with the activity and ask them to play along with the rest of the participants.

Jolt 34
Say It in Sequence

Everyone wants to be an expert. However, sometimes being an expert interferes with our ability to learn and change. In fact, resistance to change increases the more competent we become.

 ## Synopsis

Participants are asked to memorize a set of random numbers (written out) using any memorization technique they wish to use. The facilitator then asks the participants to recite the numbers from memory and then to arrange the numbers in alphabetical order to make a learning point about change.

 ## Purpose

- To explore the impact of previous learning on our current ability to learn and make changes

 ## Training Topics

- Memory
- Learning
- Change management

 ## Participants

- One or more

 ## Time

- 3 minutes for the activity
- 10 to 15 minutes for debriefing

Preparation

Here's a task for you (the facilitator) to do before the session—memorize these numbers in the following sequence. You will need this information stored in your memory at the end of the jolt. Your participants do not have to complete this task.

Eight
Five
Four
Nine
One
Seven
Six
Ten
Three
Two

Use any memorization technique you wish. I wrote down the string of numbers and memorized them as if they were a telephone number: 854–917–61032. I had to make sure that I memorized the underlined 10 as "ten" and not as "one" and "zero."

 Flow

Give instructions to count. Ask the participants to say the numbers from one to ten in sequence. As soon as the task is complete, ask the participants to stand up (and remain standing).

Give instructions to say the numbers in alphabetical order. Ask the participants to repeat the numbers from one to ten in alphabetical order (using the spelling of the number) beginning with "eight." As soon as the task is complete, ask participants to sit down. You will likely have to wait a longer time for participants to complete this task.

Demonstrate your mastery. Get the participants to pay attention as you rattle off the ten numbers in alphabetical order. Confess that you have spent a lot of time practicing this skill.

 Debriefing

Ask the participants why it took a longer time to recite the numbers in alphabetical order than in numerical order. Also ask why they made a lot more mistakes during the second activity. Use additional questions to drive home the learning points.

Ask participants for examples of old learning interfering with new. If necessary, use these examples to get them started:

- *If you have learned to drive on the right side of the road, you will have problems learning to drive in the United Kingdom, Australia, or South Africa, where people drive on the left side.*

- *During the Olympic Games in Australia, many pedestrians were killed because they crossed the road after checking the traffic coming from the left side of the road.*

- *The accent we acquire during early childhood interferes with our attempts to change it during adult life.*
- *The work styles, beliefs, and standard procedures that we learned during successful business periods interferes with our ability to change them to cope with current realities.*
- *The stereotypes that we have acquired about other races, religions, and cultures interferes with our ability to accept and accommodate global realities.*
- *If we have taught our workers to depend on us for complete directions, it is difficult for them to acquire and demonstrate initiative.*
- *If we have been taught to think in terms of linear cause-effect relationships, it is very difficult for us to acquire systems thinking.*
- *If we expect to learn from authoritative lectures, we have difficulty learning from a jolt.*

Ask participants for strategies for handling learned interference. Discuss these types of guidelines:

- *Keep an open mind about alternative approaches for achieving your goals.*
- *Be aware of your current beliefs, knowledge, and skills.*

Learning Points

1. What we have already learned interferes with what we are trying to learn afresh.
2. It is easier to learn something new if we have a blank, beginner's mind.
3. It is difficult to learn something new if we have previously learned a related skill (or knowledge or belief).

Variation

Do you want to use some other task? Instead of asking participants to count, you can use many other over-learned lists such as the days of the week or months of the year. You can also challenge participants to recite the alphabet in the reverse order.

Follow-Up

You might want to follow up this jolt with Jolt 39, Stroop, that emphasizes a similar learning point.

Jolt 35
Scrambled Words

Y ou've probably heard the popular phrase, "The devil is in the details." While this may be true, it may also be possible to become too detail-oriented. This jolt emphasizes the importance of achieving a balance (through an exaggerated example) between paying obsessive attention to details and the other extreme of ignoring them.

 ## Synopsis

Several paragraphs of scrambled text designed to test the editing and cognition skills of participants are at the heart of this jolt about focusing on the important details.

 ## Purpose

- To explore ambiguous messages and the brain's ability to fill in the blanks

 ## Training Topics

- Communication
- Mindfulness
- Writing

 ## Participants

- One or more

 ## Time

- 2 minutes for the activity
- 3 to 7 minutes for the debriefing

 ## Handout

- Scrambled Words Handout

Flow

Distribute the handout. Give each participant a copy of the handout.

Brief the participants. Tell the participants that the handout contains several typos in the form of scrambled words. Ask them to read the handout, mentally making suitable corrections to grasp the meaning of the message without trying to actually make the corrections with a pen or pencil.

Pause while participants read the handout. After 1 or 2 minutes, ask participants to stop reading and proceed to the debriefing discussion.

 Debriefing

Conduct a debriefing discussion using the following questions:

- *Is the relevancy of a message more important than the clarity? For example, would you abandon trying to understand an unclear ransom note from someone who had kidnapped your wife, child, relative, colleague, or significant other?*

- *What implications does your brain's tendency to ignore errors and understand the main message have for the written materials used in your profession?*

- *How correct are the grammar, syntax, and spelling in your written messages? More importantly, how important is correctness (grammatical or otherwise) to your audience? Does this audience care about the miniscule details of accuracy?*

- *Younger people have grown up with text messages and other cryptic ways of communicating. How do you think a member of this generation would react to the scrambled words in the handout? How would a member of an older generation react to this handout?*

- *Accuracy is very important to people working in some professions. For example, lawyers (words and language) or accountants (numbers) must pay attention to these details. Pop or rap musicians are clearly not concerned about grammatical accuracy. What is the appropriate level of accuracy for your profession?*

 Learning Points

1. If it's not important to your audience, don't obsess too much about accuracy and grammatical correctness.
2. If your audience is motivated by the message they will ignore any errors.

 Variation

You don't like our handout? Go to the website http://www.lerfjhax.com/scrambler and create your own scrambled word message that is more relevant for your participants.

Scrambled Words Handout

Your Brian Is Smrat!

Tihs is not eaxctly a pzzlue but an inttreeinsg dnteosaiortmn of the biran's ali-itby to mkae maening out of slebcmrad and jlbmeud wodrs, as lnog as the fisrt and the lsat ltetres are in thier ccorert ptosioin.

I use tehse senetnces to dmtsonreate how sarmt the biarn is.

Wtrires sepnd a lot of tmie mnkiag srue taht tiher winritg is caelr and esay to udntanserd. But a mtietvoad radeer can undrentasd yuor massgee mcuh mroe eilsay tahn you bveilee.

Retcenly, I drseoievcd tihs Wrod Scmablrer wbetsie wrehe you can go and tpye a mgsasee wtih clcreroty slepeld wdros: http://www.lerfjhax.com/scrambler. (Don't wrroy. The URL is not smclrbaed.) The prargom semlacrbs the leertts in ecah wrod (lnvaieg the fisrt and the lsat ltetres in tiher ccorert litnacoos) as you tpye! You can cut and ptsae the sacbelmrd wdors to certae yuor datostmenoirn magesse.

Jolt 36
Sequencing

Integrating bits of information into a meaningful sequence is a useful strategy for memorization because it is easier to recall things that make sense to you. This activity dramatically demonstrates the effectiveness of sequencing.

 ## Synopsis

Participants are given a short time to memorize a list of words and then are instructed to recall as many words as possible. This memorization test highlights the importance of making use of meaningful sequences.

 ## Purpose

- To show how the sequencing of words is connected to meaning and memory

 ## Training Topics

- Memory
- Communication
- Writing

 ## Caution

As noted in other similar activities, don't give away the trick of this jolt by distributing the handouts from two stacks. Mix the two versions of the handout before coming to the session.

 ## Participants

- Two or more

 ## Time

- 3 minutes for the activity
- 5 to 10 minutes for debriefing

Supplies

- Paper
- Pens or pencils
- Countdown timer
- Whistle

Handouts

- Two different versions of the Memory Test Handout

Flow

Brief participants. Tell the participants that you plan to administer a simple memory test. Distribute a word list to each participant from the two versions you prepared previously. Make sure that equal numbers of the two versions are used. Ask participants not to read the lists and to hold the lists with printed side down until you give instructions.

Conduct the memorization exercise. Tell the participants they will have 40 seconds to memorize the words on the list. Blow your whistle to signal the start of the test. After 40 seconds, blow the whistle again to conclude the test. Ask the participants to place the word lists on the table (or their laps) with the printed side down.

Conduct the recall exercise. Distribute blank sheets of paper to each participant. Ask them to think about the words they memorized on the handout and to list as many as possible, one word per line, in any order. Announce a 1-minute time limit. While the participants are constructing their lists, pick up the handout word lists.

Score the recalled words. After 1 minute, blow your whistle and ask participants to exchange their word lists with other participants for scoring and tell them each word recalled is worth 1 point. Then read the list of words below:

a
ability
aliens
amazing
at
by
have
just
lemon
sourness
staring
strange
taste
the
to
yellow

Identify high scoring participants. Ask your participants to identify themselves as you count down from the maximum number of correct answers (16) until all the participants have responded. Locate the top 5 to 10 scores.

Reveal the secret. Reveal to the participants that you passed out two versions of the word lists, one with a list of random words in alphabetical order and the other version with the same words arranged in a sequence to form a sentence.

 ## Debriefing

Conduct a discussion about why it is easier to recall words from the list that formed a sentence than from the handout with just a list of words. Ask questions to help participants conclude that arranging words in an appropriate sequence gives them meaning. Discuss the implications of this principle beyond this exercise.

 ## Learning Points

1. Sentences are easier to remember than a list of disconnected words.
2. Our communication will be clearer and easier to remember if we arrange our sentences and ideas in a meaningful sequence.

 ## Variation

You don't like the sentence? Write a sentence that is more relevant to your instructional topic or your organization. Prepare the second list by using the same words in alphabetical order.

 ## Field Notes

Participants recall about 12 words from the sentence on average and 7 words from the alphabetical list.

Follow-Up

Another jolt, Jolt 24, Memory Test, deals with a similar topic and uses a similar approach. You might use this jolt before or after Memory Test to present a related set of learning points.

Memory Test Handout

Here is a sentence that is printed one word per line. Memorize the sentence:

strange
aliens
have
the
amazing
ability
to
taste
sourness
just
by
staring
at
a
yellow
lemon

Memory Test Handout

Here are words of different lengths printed in alphabetical order. Memorize the words:

a
ability
aliens
amazing
at
by
have
just
lemon
sourness
staring
strange
taste
the
to
yellow

Jolt 37
Shapes and Colors

Jumping to conclusions is a common mistake that people make. This jolt demonstrates the causes and consequences of such impulsive decision making.

 Synopsis

A volunteer participant is tasked with picking out only red triangle pieces from a grocery bag. The volunteer assumes the task is possible even with closed eyes based on the information about the contents of the bag provided by the facilitator. The faulty assumption provides valuable learning opportunities for the participants.

 Purpose

- To explore the impact of hasty generalizations and the hazards of making decisions based on partial information

 Training Topics

- Critical thinking
- Stereotyping

 Participants

- Two or more
- A volunteer participates in the activity while the others watch

 Time

- 3 minutes for the activity
- 5 minutes for debriefing

Supplies

- Twenty-four rectangular and triangular pieces cut from red and blue card stock (see Preparation below for details)
- A grocery bag

 Caution

Since the jolt involves asking a volunteer to close her eyes and perform a task, select someone who can handle playful kidding to be your volunteer. After the session, point out that the inability to do the task was not the volunteer's fault.

 Preparation

Cut sheets of red and blue card stock to create twenty-four colored pieces as listed below:

- Six red rectangles
- Six blue rectangles
- Six red triangles
- Six blue triangles

Place these pieces inside a large grocery bag.

 Flow

Show the cardboard pieces. Reach inside the grocery bag you brought to the session and pull out a red rectangle piece and a blue triangle piece. Show the pieces to all participants. Use a script similar to the one below to reveal the bag's contents:

"This bag contains twenty-four pieces of cardboard I have cut into two types of shapes—rectangles and triangles—using two colors—red and blue. Here is a red rectangle and here is a blue triangle."

Your job is to encourage participants to assume that all rectangles are red and all triangles are blue. You are not being untruthful, just leaving out some important details.

Invite a volunteer. Invite a participant to come to the front of the room and tell her that the activity involves selecting only red pieces with closed eyes. (The volunteer will assume this is easy since she believes all the rectangles are red, so feeling for the shape of the cardboard piece will lead to success.)

Begin the activity. Do not let the volunteer see the pieces inside the grocery bag. Ask the volunteer to close her eyes, reach inside the bag, and pick seven red pieces, one at a time. When the volunteer gives you the pieces, hold them up so that the audience members can see them. Make sure their reaction does not let the volunteer know something is not right. Place your finger on your lips to signal to the audience to be silent.

Jolts! Activities to Wake Up and Engage Your Participants

Conclude the activity. Conclude the activity when your volunteer has given you seven pieces. Then ask the volunteer to open her eyes and reveal the pieces she selected. The pieces will be a mix of red and blue rectangles. Playfully complain, "But I wanted you to select red pieces. What are the blue pieces doing here?"

Debriefing

What did you learn? Conduct a discussion with all participants to elicit the following conclusions:

- In this activity, sight is a more useful sense than touch.
- After seeing a red rectangle, everyone jumped to the conclusion that all rectangles were red.

Ask the participants how they might change their future behaviors based on what happened. Use follow-up questions that elicit responses about the lessons learned in this activity and how they might be used in their workplace.

Learning Points

1. Hasty, incorrect conclusions are often based on incomplete information.
2. Incorrect, stereotypical conclusions about people are often made in haste and not based on full information.
3. Before we can really understand other human beings, we need a lot more information other than just external appearance.

Variation

Volunteer hesitates and says there could be rectangles of both colors. Congratulate the volunteer on her critical thinking skills and ask her to try anyway with her eyes closed. During the debriefing, once again comment on the volunteer's logic and ask how many people had not made the expected assumption.

Field Notes

This is how you can make sure that you pick the right pieces in the beginning: Before the session, pick a red rectangle and a blue triangle and paper clip them together. Drop this pair of cutouts inside the grocery bag. At the beginning of the session, grope inside the bag until you feel the paper clip and remove it before bringing out the rectangle and triangle pieces.

Jolt 38
Six Tiles

A serial jolt repeats the same type of jolt several times with slight variations. Six Tiles is an interesting example of a serial jolt that repeatedly entraps participants into making unwarranted assumptions, even though they are warned against making these assumptions.

Synopsis

Participants arrange lettered tile sets projected on a screen so that the tiles spell words. The words must be formed following specific rules provided by the facilitator. However, the participants make assumptions during each round of play that makes it difficult if not impossible to succeed at the task.

Purpose

- To increase awareness about the assumptions we make

Training Topics

- Problem solving
- Creative thinking
- Critical thinking

Participants

- One or more

Time

- 2 minutes for each round
- 15 to 20 minutes for all rounds, including debriefing

Facilitator's Note

A set of twenty-nine slides (Six Tiles.ppt) is required for this jolt. These can be found at www.pfeiffer.com/go/jolts.

Equipment

- Laptop computer
- LCD projector
- Screen

Caution

This jolt repeatedly traps participants into making mistakes. Your participants may feel frustrated and irritated, so maintain a playful attitude. If necessary, present the jolt as a narrative of how you were entrapped into making unnecessary assumptions, one after another.

Preparation

Copy the slides to your laptop computer or a zip drive. Connect to an LCD projector and click through the slides. Try to experience the activity from the point of view of a participant and what happens during the seven rounds.

Flow

Brief the participants. Project Slide 1 and explain to your participants that the activity is called Six Tiles because the slides used for the activity display six tiles with three letters printed on each of the tiles. Project Slide 2 and read the simple instruction: *Rearrange the six tiles to spell three words*.

Introduce an easy task. Project Slide 3 containing these tiles:

MAN   LES   OBJ   AGE   SON   ECT

Note that this round is a practice round to help participants understand the requirements and process for solving the puzzle. After a brief pause, display Slide 4 with the correct answer:

MANAGE   LESSON   OBJECT

Demonstrate the first assumption. Project the instruction again (Slide 5) and then show Slide 6 with these tiles:

ATT   END   RET   ION   RIT   IRE

Give the participants about 30 seconds as they struggle to make three words out of these six tiles. After about 30 seconds, project Slide 7 with this answer:

ATTRITION   RETIRE   END

Follow up with a quick debriefing. Point out that the participants made an assumption that the three words must all be six letters long based on the sample solution given previously.

Demonstrate the second assumption. Project the instructions again (Slide 8) and then show Slide 9 with these tiles:

AMI   EEF   LIA   RDS   RWO   THR

After about 30 seconds, Project Slide 10 with this answer:

THREEFAMILIARWORDS

Point out during another quick debriefing that the participants made an assumption (based on the earlier rounds) that the correct solution contained three words with no spaces between the words.

Demonstrate the third assumption. Project the instruction slide once again (Slide 11) and then show Slide 12 with these tiles:

ACT   FAT   HER   NIH   NOI   WIT

After about 30 seconds, project Slide 13 with this answer:

FATHER   ACTION   WITHIN

After an inevitable howl of protest, project Slides 14 and 15 to show how two of the tiles were turned upside down to change the sequence of letters:

NIH → HIN
NOI → ION

Make sure that the participants understand the strategy now and point out how the assumption that the tiles could not be turned around led to their difficulty in solving the puzzle.

Demonstrate the fourth assumption. Project the instruction slide again (Slide 16) and then show Slide 17 with these tiles:

ONE   WAY   HOW   ANY   THI   ACP

After about 30 seconds, project Slide 18 with this answer:

ANYONE   ANYHOW   ANYWAY

During another quick debriefing, point out that the participants made two assumptions. One, that all tiles have to be used and, two, that the participants were not allowed to use any tiles more than once.

Demonstrate the fifth assumption. Project Slide 19 (the instruction slide) and then show Slide 20 with these tiles:

ARL   TAI   TCG   EKH   NET   DTS

After about 30 seconds, project Slide 21 with this answer:

A R L
T A I
T C G
E K H
N E T
D T S

Point out to the participants during another quick debriefing that they might not be able to see the three words immediately because of another assumption—that the words are arranged to be read from left to right. Suggest reading vertically from top to bottom so that these words are revealed: *attend, racket, and lights*.

Demonstrate the sixth assumption. Project the instruction slide (Slide 22) and then show Slide 23 with these tiles:

MAI   VAL   SON   GAR   CHE   CON

After about 30 seconds, project Slide 24 with this answer:

MAISON   GARCON   CHEVAL

During this debriefing discussion point out to the participants that they made an assumption that only words in English were permitted. Ask whether anyone recognizes these French words for *house, boy, and horse*.

Demonstrate the seventh assumption. Project Slide 25 with these new instructions: *Rearrange the letters from the six tiles to spell six-letter words*. Very few participants will read or notice the new instructions.

Project Slide 26 containing these tiles:

DEN   HAL   LET   OUT   TED   TER

After about 30 seconds, project Slide 27 containing nearly two hundred six-letter words.

Point out that the participants assumed the instructions were the same as before and didn't notice the change. Project Slide 28 with the new instructions and point out that the instructions directed the participants to rearrange the *letters* and not the *tiles*.

 ## Debriefing

You conducted debriefing discussions for this jolt during the activity at the end of each round (in a just-in-time fashion). Here are some additional points to include at the end of the series.

Apologize and thank participants. Apologize to the participants about the series of frustrating and irritating activities. Thank all the participants for playing along with you and for being good sports.

Ask participants to apply their insights. Invite participants to pair up with each other and ask them to discuss a workplace problem they are trying to solve. Encourage the partners to help each other uncover unnecessary assumptions that might be counter-productive to finding a solution.

 ## Learning Points

1. Everyone makes a lot of counterproductive, unwarranted assumptions during problem-solving activities.
2. Even an awareness of our tendency to make unwarranted assumptions does not prevent us from continuing to make these assumptions.
3. One way to avoid assumptions is to reflect on this predisposition and to learn from our mistakes.

Variation

You don't have enough time? Just conduct a couple of rounds. Speed through the other slides and explain the assumptions made.

Field Notes

This is an activity that grew from a single round. Many readers of our online newsletter and participants in our workshops contributed some of the twists that became later rounds. If you have your own diabolical ideas on how to enhance this activity with some new tempting traps, please send a note to tracy@thiagi.com.

Jolt 39
Stroop

It is difficult to change behaviors that are ingrained and automatic, especially skills-based behavior patterns, which are nearly impossible to turn off. For example, you cannot look at printed text without automatically reading it. You read the text and cannot force yourself to see just lines and shapes. This jolt is a powerful demonstration of the difficulty of changing skilled behaviors.

 ## Synopsis

Participants are asked to alternately read words and name the font colors, demonstrating the difficulty of changing patterns of automatic responses.

 ## Purpose

- To explore how previous learning can interfere with new learning

 ## Training Topics

- Learning
- Memory
- Change management

 ## Participants

- One or more

 ## Time

- 3 minutes for the activity
- 3 to 7 minutes for debriefing

Facilitator's Note

A set of four slides (Stroop.ppt) is used for this jolt. They can be found at www.pfeiffer .com/go/jolts.

Equipment

- Laptop computer
- LCD projector
- Screen

Preparation

Copy the slides to your laptop computer or zip drive. Connect to an LCD projector and click through the slides to ensure proper sequencing.

Flow

Brief the participants. Tell the participants about the Stroop activity and point out that the activity is called Stroop because it is named after John Ridley Stroop, a psychologist who first demonstrated this interesting effect in 1935.

Ask participants to read the words. Project Slide 1 containing the names of different colors printed in black font. Ask participants to read the words rapidly out loud.

Ask participants to name the font colors. Project Slide 2 displaying a list of unpronounceable letter sets and ask participants to *say the name of the font color* of each letter set out loud.

Demonstrate the Stroop effect. Project Slide 3, containing the words for a series of colors, but this time printed in a different color than described by the word (for example, the word *Red* is printed in blue). Watch the participants stumble through naming the font colors. The time required to complete this task will be significantly longer than the time taken to read the black-and-white version of color names displayed in the first slide.

Debriefing

During the debriefing relate the activity to resistance to change of any kind. Note that we experience this resistance when we are asked to switch to a new software program, for example. Even a professional tennis player asked to modify a serving technique experiences the same resistance to change.

Learning Points

1. Changing our habits is difficult.
2. Avoiding using a well-learned and practiced skill is especially difficult.

Variation

You don't want to use a computer? Use a flip chart and color markers. Copy the content and the colors of the three slides on three separate flip-chart pages.

Field Notes

Many websites have demonstrations of the Stroop effect. You can learn more about the original experiments and later enhancements in many places, including this Wikipedia article (http://en.wikipedia.org/wiki/Stroop_effect).

Follow-Up

Jolt 34, Say It in Sequence, presents a similar learning point and is a good follow-up to this activity.

Jolt 40
Synchronized Clapping

This jolt emphasizes the difference between understanding something and applying that learning. It is perhaps our favorite jolt.

 ## Synopsis

Participants learn the difficulty of listening and following directions required for even simple activities such as clapping their hands simultaneously.

 ## Purpose

- To emphasize that actions speak louder than words

 ## Training Topics

- Leadership
- Learning

 ## Participants

- Any number over ten
- This activity works best with groups of ten to one hundred

 ## Time

- 2 minutes for the activity
- 3 to 10 minutes for debriefing

 ## Flow

Conduct a practice round. Ask all the participants to clap their hands once. Pause while participants do this.

203

Brief the participants. Complain that the participants' clapping was ragged and unimpressive and that you want them to synchronize their claps so that those outside the room hear a single thunderous sound.

Provide performance support. Explain that you will provide a non-electronic performance support system to synchronize all the participants' claps: you will count "One, two, three" and then say, "Clap." Ask everyone in the room to wait until you say, "Clap" before they clap simultaneously.

Conduct the activity. Count out loud, "One, two, three." Immediately after you say "three," clap your hands (without saying the word "Clap"). Most participants will follow your lead and clap their hands as well. Act surprised and say, "Clap."

 ## Debriefing

Ask the participants why they did not follow your instructions and wait until they heard the word "Clap" before clapping hands. Some participant will likely say, "But you clapped your hands. . . ." They will likely anticipate your response, "Would you jump off a cliff if I did?"

Ask the participants what they learned from the activity. Discuss the learning points that the participants offer.

 ## Learning Points

1. Actions speak louder than words.
2. People follow your actions more than your words.
3. A big gap exists between understanding instructions and following them.

 ## Field Notes

This is an effective jolt to use near the beginning of a training session. If this jolt follows other jolts, participants may suspect that you are planning to trap them and avoid following your lead.

Jolt 41
Team Planning

Here's a jolt that explores how people plan to complete team projects.

Synopsis

Participants form teams and devise a strategy to work cooperatively to solve a series of micro-Sudoku puzzles. The jolt concludes with a discussion of team strategies and learning points gained from the activity.

Purpose

- To explore how teams can work together to complete a challenging activity

Training Topics

- Teamwork
- Planning

Participants

- Six or more
- The best number of participants is between twelve and thirty

Time

- 3 minutes for the activity
- 5 to 10 minutes for debriefing

Supplies

- One copy of How to Solve Micro-Sudoku Puzzles for the facilitator
- Countdown timer
- Whistle

- Flip chart
- Felt-tipped pens

 Preparation

Read the facilitator handout. Review the contents of the facilitator handout to become familiar with solving micro-Sudoku puzzles.

Draw the following micro-Sudoku puzzle on a flip chart:

		4	
	2		3
2			
	4		1

 Flow

Brief the players. Ask how many participants have previously solved Sudoku puzzles. Tell the participants that most people are familiar with the 9 by 9 Sudoku grids. Point out that for this activity, you will use an easier 4 by 4 micro-Sudoku grid.

Explain how to solve the puzzle. Using the micro-Sudoku grid that you prepared on the flip chart, explain that the puzzle is solved by placing one number (1, 2, 3, or 4) in each of the boxes so that each column, each row, and each 2 by 2 block (outlined with a heavy line) includes all four numbers. Use a felt-tipped marker of a different color than you used to draw the Sudoku grid and engage participants in the process of solving the puzzle.

Organize participants into teams. After demonstrating how to solve the puzzle, organize participants into teams of two to five members (it does not matter if a few teams have one more member than the other teams).

Explain the team challenge. Explain the challenge to the participants. Tell them that they will receive a set of thirty micro-Sudoku puzzles and that each team will work together to solve as many Sudoku puzzles as possible. However, before the activity begins, each team will have 3 minutes to plan the best strategy to complete the task.

Conduct the planning activity. Set your countdown timer for 3 minutes and start it. Encourage the teams to engage everyone in the process of planning their puzzle-solving strategy. Remind the participants of the 3-minute time limit for this planning.

Conclude the planning activity. Blow your whistle at the end of 3 minutes and announce the end of the planning period. Randomly select a team and ask for a spokesperson to present the highlights of their plan. Ask the spokespersons from the other teams to present any additional strategies discussed in their teams.

Debriefing

Invite participants to comment on and discuss the similarities and differences between the different team strategies and approaches. Continue with discussion uses questions such as:

- *Did you have enough time for planning?*
- *How many of you felt that planning did not add value in this situation?*
- *The team challenge involved a novel activity. Is planning more important or less important when you have this type of novel activity?*
- *The team challenge involved a specific time-bound activity. Is planning more important or less important when you have this type of specific activity?*
- *Did you plan to assign different responsibilities to different members of the team? If so, how did you make this decision?*
- *How did different members of your team participate in the planning activity?*
- *What are some possible reasons for different levels of participation among team members?*
- *How did your planning procedure resemble other planning activities in your workplace?*
- *If you were to conduct the planning activity again, how would you do it differently?*
- *Are you planning to add ideas from the other teams to your team's plan?*
- *Did you discuss the advantages and disadvantages of each team member working alone on a puzzle assigned to him or her, two team members tackling the same puzzle, or all team members tackling the same puzzle?*

Learning Points

1. Approaches to planning varies widely among people and teams.
2. Some people prefer action instead of planning and see little value in the planning activity.

Variation

Don't feel comfortable explaining how to solve the puzzles? Make copies of the handout, How to Solve Micro-Sudoku Puzzles. Distribute copies of the handout to participants at the start of this activity and devise a solution strategy together.

Follow-Up

When we use this jolt as a stand-alone activity, some participants are disappointed because they expected an opportunity to solve the puzzles. You might address this issue by using a follow-up, Jolt 42, Teamwork, that involves actually solving mini-Sudoku puzzles. However, don't skip the debriefing activity specified for this jolt. Pairing the two jolts elicits interesting and useful insights about planning and strategic thinking.

How to Solve Micro-Sudoku Puzzles

Sudoku puzzles (with 9 by 9 grids) show up everywhere: airline magazines, newspapers, websites, and in books. If you are intimidated by these puzzles and avoid them or like them so much that you worry about becoming addicted to them, we have just the thing for you: *micro-Sudoku puzzles* that use less complex 4 by 4 grids.

Here's a sample micro-Sudoku puzzle:

	1		
2	4		
		1	
			2

To solve the puzzle, you must place the numbers (1, 2, 3, or 4) in each of the blank boxes so that each number appears only once in each column, each row, and in each 2 by 2 block (which is surrounded by thicker lines).

Given this requirement, you should be able to solve the puzzle logically. However, if you need some help, observe me as I figure out the placement of a few of the numbers. Follow the step-by-step progression as the answer emerges and I place the number in the gray box that follows:

3	1		
2	4		
		1	
			2

3	1		
2	4		1
		1	
			2

3	1		
2	4	3	1
		1	
			2

3	1	2	
2	4	3	1
		1	
			2

You should be able to figure out the rest of the solution, but here's the final solution.

3	1	2	4
2	4	3	1
4	2	1	3
1	3	4	2

Jolt 42
Team Power

Teams are often able to outperform any one of their individual members. This jolt is a demonstration of the power of teams.

 Synopsis

Participants work independently and as teams to solve word puzzles and learn how combining the work and brainpower of individual players produces greater and more productive results.

 Purpose

- To demonstrate the difference between team and individual performance

 Training Topics

- Teamwork
- Cooperation
- Diversity

 Participants

- Six or more
- This jolt works best with twelve or more participants

 Time

- 3 minutes for the activity
- 5 to 10 minutes for debriefing

 Supplies

- Countdown timer
- Whistle

Handouts

- A set of twelve word puzzles (Handout 1). Provide one copy for each participant plus an extra copy for each team.
- A Team Power Puzzles Solutions handout for the facilitator

Preparation

Make copies of the word puzzle handout. Imagine yourself as a participant and try to solve as many of the puzzles as possible and study the solutions.

Flow

Brief the participants. Distribute copies of the handout containing twelve word puzzles and ask whether anyone is familiar with puzzles of this type. Ask the participants to study the first puzzle and the solution.

Explain the activity. Tell the participants that they will work independently for the next 2 minutes to solve as many of the word puzzles as possible.

Conduct the activity. Set your countdown timer for 2 minutes. Blow your whistle and ask participants to begin solving the puzzles as you start the timer. After 2 minutes, tell participants to stop working.

Organize participants into teams. Ask the participants to form teams of three to six people each.

Ask teams to combine their solutions. Provide a new copy of the puzzle handout to each team. Tell the individual team members not to change or work on their individual puzzle sheets. Instead, explain that all the team members will incorporate their individual answers into a new team puzzle sheet.

Compare individual and team scores. You should find that the team score is greater than (or equal to) the best individual scores attained by team members. Ask the team members to compare and contrast their solutions for the different word puzzles.

Debriefing

Ask questions such as:

- *What did you learn from this activity?*
- *How many of you prefer solving word puzzles independently and how many of you prefer solving them as a team?*
- *How would you feel if your team did not contribute any additional solutions to what you had independently solved?*
- *How would you feel if you had solved one or more of the puzzles that nobody in your group had solved?*
- *What types of workplace activities benefit from teamwork?*

Learning Points

1. In most cases, teams working together outperform the efforts of individual members.
2. Not all activities require teamwork, and some activities benefit more than others from using a team approach.
3. Not all people prefer to work in a team.

Variations

You don't like word puzzles? Instead of the puzzles, use a set of trivia questions from appropriate bodies of knowledge.

You are working with a non-English speaking group? Use some other type of non-verbal puzzle. We have used picture puzzles in which participants try to locate different hidden objects. We have also used two pictures and required participants to find subtle differences in the pictures while working as a team.

NOON GOOD

Good afternoon

DEILST

ME QUIT

DCTNRY

BOJACKX

WORL

CARNREATION

SYMPHON

ARREST
YOU ARE

TRN

TIMING
TIM ING

I AM YOU

Team Power Puzzles Solutions

GOOD AFTERNOON	REINCARNATION
LISTED IN ALPHABETICAL ORDER	UNFINISHED SYMPHONY
QUIT FOLLOWING ME	YOU ARE UNDER ARREST
ABRIDGED DICTIONARY	NO U-TURN
JACK IN THE BOX	SPLIT SECOND TIMING
WORLD WITHOUT END	I AM BIGGER THAN YOU

Jolt 43
Teamwork

This jolt explores how people work together to complete team projects. You can use this jolt as a follow-up to Jolt 41, Team Planning.

 ## Synopsis

Participants must solve a number of micro-Sudoku puzzles and use the power of teamwork to get the task done and beat a time limit of 3 minutes

 ## Purpose

- To demonstrate the power of teams working together to complete a challenging activity

 ## Training Topics

- Teamwork
- Planning
- Cooperation

 ## Participants

- Six or more
- The best number of participants is twelve to thirty

 ## Time

- 3 minutes for the activity
- 5 to 10 minutes for debriefing

 ## Supplies

- Countdown timer
- Whistle

Handout

- A collection of thirty micro-Sudoku puzzles (Teamwork Handout 1), one copy for each participant

Facilitator's Note

Conduct Jolt 41, Team Planning, and debrief the participants before conducting this jolt.

Flow

Distribute the puzzles. Give each participant a copy the handout containing thirty micro-Sudoku puzzles with the printed side facing down. Tell the participants not to look at the puzzles yet.

Brief the participants. Inform the participants they will have 3 minutes to *work as a team* to solve as many puzzles as possible. Have them form small teams if they are not already in table groups. Note that working as a team does not require all team members to focus on or participate in solving *each* puzzle.

Conduct the puzzle-solving activity. Set your countdown timer for 2 minutes and start it. Tell the teams to begin solving the puzzles and remind them that they have 3 minutes to work on this activity.

Conclude the puzzle-solving activity. Blow your whistle after 3 minutes to announce the end of the puzzle-solving period. Ask each team to count the total number of puzzles they solved and ask team members to call out this total. Identify the highest scoring team and congratulate the team members.

Debriefing

Conduct a discussion with the participants asking questions such as:

- *Did you consider yourself competing with the other teams? How did this competition influence your teamwork?*
- *How do you feel about the team that solved the most puzzles? What do you think is the secret of their success?*
- *Did the team members work individually or as a team?*
- *How did you divide the task among different members of the team?*
- *What interesting things did you learn about your teammates?*
- *How did you coordinate the activities of different team members?*
- *Did anyone take charge of the team?*
- *How much time was spent in coordinating the teamwork? How much time was spent in the actual puzzle-solving activity?*
- *Did the task of solving the puzzles lend itself to teamwork?*
- *Which would have been more productive: five people working individually in solving the puzzles or five people working together as a team?*

Jolts! Activities to Wake Up and Engage Your Participants

- *If you were to repeat the puzzle-solving activity, what recommendations would you make to your team?*

- *In what ways does the puzzle-solving activity reflect team activities in your workplace?*

Learning Points

1. All well-laid plans are subject to the impact of reality.
2. Planning is time well spent, but strict adherence to a plan invites problems.
3. Flexible plans make room for new opportunities.

Variation

Do you want to use this as a stand-alone jolt? If you want to skip the Team Planning jolt, make copies of the handout, How to Solve Micro-Sudoku Puzzles (presented in Jolt 41) and distribute one copy to each participant. Give the participants a couple of minutes to read the handout and figure out how to solve the puzzles; then distribute the puzzle sheets to begin the activity. Follow the same debriefing plan.

Field Notes

In our experience, the number of different puzzles solved by teams of five members ranges from nine to fifteen. The current record is twenty-one puzzles. Do not worry about your teams running out of puzzles to solve during the 3-minute period.

Teamwork Handout 1

Row 1

Grid 1:
	4	3	
4	3	2	

Grid 2:
	3		2
1	4		

Grid 3:
4		1	
		2	
1	3		

Grid 4:
		1	
	4		
2			
		3	

Grid 5:
			1
	4		
		1	3

Row 2

Grid 1:
	2	1	
	4		
2			

Grid 2:
	2		
1			
	3		
		4	

Grid 3:
3			
			2
	4	1	

Grid 4:
	2		
1		3	
		4	
	3		

Grid 5:
		4	
2			
			3
	3		

Row 3

Grid 1:
	3	4	
	2	1	

Grid 2:
		3	4
4	1		

Grid 3:
1			
3	1		
			4

Grid 4:
			4
		2	
	1		
2	4		

Grid 5:
	4		
	3		
	4		
	2		

Row 4

Grid 1:
	1		
	2	4	
4			1

Grid 2:
			3
1			
2	1		
1			

Grid 3:
		4	2
		2	
	3		

Grid 4:
	3		
2		3	
		1	
	2		

Grid 5:
		1	
	2		
1		3	

Row 5

Grid 1:
	1		
	4		
2			
			3

Grid 2:
		2	4
		4	
1			

Grid 3:
	4		1
		1	
3			

Grid 4:
3			
	2		
		4	1
			3

Grid 5:
	1		3
		4	
2	1		

Row 6

Grid 1:
	2		
2			1
3			

Grid 2:
			1
	4		
	2	4	

Grid 3:
	1		
4			
		4	3
			1

Grid 4:
3			2
			4
1			

Grid 5:
	4	3	1
	3	4	

Jolt 44
The Training Story

How often do you wonder whether someone is really listening to you or just thinking about what they are going to say next? This jolt emphasizes the importance of developing good listening skills. It also highlights the importance of clear goals.

 ## Synopsis

Participants are asked to listen to a recording of a story. The participants assume that they are to listen closely and solve a mathematical problem. However, they learn at the end of the activity that solving the problem was not the real point.

 ## Purpose

- To demonstrate the importance of good listening skills

 ## Training Topics

- Communication
- Goal focus

 ## Participants

- One or more

 ## Time

- 3 minutes for the activity
- 5 to 7 minutes for the debriefing

Facilitator's Note

This jolt uses an audio recording (Training Story.mp3) found at www.pfeiffer.com/go/jolts.

Equipment

- Laptop computer
- Speakers

 ## Preparation

Copy the mp3 file to your computer or zip drive. Ensure that your audio equipment is operational.

 ## Caution

During the debriefing, some participants may claim that you did in fact ask for a solution, so you may have to replay instructions on the audio recording.

 ## Flow

Play the audio recording. Here is the content of this recording:

- *Let's do a mathematical problem to see how good you are with using information received.*
- *Imagine this…*
- *You enter a training room where six other learners have already begun working individually on an e-learning program.*
- *After 10 minutes, two learners leave.*
- *After 20 minutes, two more learners leave.*
- *After 30 minutes, no one leaves, but three learners enter the room.*
- *Four learners leave at the break.*
- *When the break is over, three learners return.*
- *After an hour, two more learners enter the training room.*
- *When the day is over, six learners leave.*
- *Without communicating to anyone next to you, jot down what you came up with.*
- *What did you come up with?*
- *Zero? No one is left?*

 ## Debriefing

Conduct a debriefing discussion, using this script:

- *What was my question? Did I ask a question?*
- *No! I said, "Let's do a mathematical problem to see how good you are with using information received."*

- *However, I didn't ask a question. What were you answering?*

- *What we did was human nature: We assumed that the question would be, "How many people are left in the training room?" If I had asked that question, you were right if you said, "No one."*

- *But, I didn't ask that question. I could have asked, "How many times did learners enter or leave the training room?"*

Continue to probe with more questions to elicit the learning points.

Learning Points

1. We are often in such a hurry to answer that we are not really listening.
2. We all use selective listening and make assumptions to fill in the gaps.
3. When no goals are provided (or vague goals) the results are inconsistent.

Variations

Would you like a more relevant story? Come up with a business narrative that is related to your organization or industry.

You don't have computers and speakers? Just read the script.

Field Notes

Participants typically have answers ranging from zero to three people left in the training room. On rare occasions, a few people may even say that they have no answer because there was no question in the first place.

Jolt 45
Visualize a Tree

This jolt demonstrates that thinking in pictures is a universal phenomenon. We have conducted the jolt around the world and have consistently arrived at the same conclusion: Most people think and process information with images, not words.

 ## Synopsis

Participants are asked to visualize "tree." The participants discover during the debriefing that different people visualized different trees and not the letters of the word "tree."

 ## Purpose

- To emphasize that the mind is oriented to think visually

 ## Training Topics

- Communication
- Memory
- Learning

 ## Participants

- One or more participants

 ## Time

- 1 minute for the activity
- 5 to 10 minutes for debriefing

 ## Flow

Set up. Tell the participants that this activity requires them to close their eyes and think about a familiar word.

Conduct the visualization activity. Ask participants to close their eyes. Say the word "Tree" and ask the participants to visualize the object.

Conclude the activity. Instruct the participants to open their eyes when they have a clear image of "tree" in their minds.

Debriefing

Ask four or five randomly selected participants what kind of tree they saw in their mind's eye. Repeat the answers for the other participants, stressing the variety of trees that the participants mention.

Ask the participants whether they visualized a generic tree or a specific tree (such as one that grows in someone's yard). Select a few participants to answer the question and then explore why different people have different preferences in this visualization exercise.

Ask the participants whether anyone visualized the letters T-R-E-E in the mind's eye. Act surprised when no one says he or she saw the letters.

Learning Points

1. Most people are visually oriented.
2. We all visualize the same object in different ways.

Variation

Do you want to pursue this topic further? Ask the participants how they would visualize abstract concepts such as *justice* or *return on investment*. Ask them to close their eyes and visualize an abstract concept that you specify.

Field Notes

The specific types of trees differ, but most people around the world think in pictures, not in words.

Jolt 46
What's Funny?

Perhaps our secret to humor lies in the ability to find humor in the events that we see and live every day. Here is a jolt that can be used to increase your own ability to find humor and joy in ordinary events.

 ## Synopsis

Participants are asked to find round objects in the immediate surroundings. This activity is used as a springboard to find humor in overlooked events and circumstances of life.

 ## Purpose

- To expand the ability of participants to find the humor in ordinary events

 ## Training Topics

- Playfulness
- Happiness

 ## Participants

- One or more
- The best group size for this activity is ten to twenty participants

 ## Time

- 3 to 5 minutes for the activity
- 7 to 15 minutes for debriefing

Flow

Ask participants to find circular objects. Say something like this:

Quick, look around you and find all the circular objects you can spot. Work silently and without help from anyone else. Identify as many objects as you can within the next 20 seconds.

Explain the point. Pause for 20 seconds. Get the participants' attention and say that the exact number of circular objects does not matter. Point out that the participants did not create these circular objects and, because the objects already existed in their environmental landscape, all the participants did was to find the objects and focus their attention on them.

Conduct a quick debrief. Conduct a quick debriefing discussion using questions such as:

- *Did you "cheat" by including parts of noncircular objects?*
- *Did you count the same object twice, as in the case of a round CD and a round hole in the middle of the CD?*
- *Did you treat an oval as a circle, as in the case of the buttons on your cell phone?*
- *Did you count multiple occurrences of the same object, as in the case of all of the periods in a printed handout?*

Reassure participants they are not cheating. Say that using this "higher level of vigilance" was not cheating.

Ask participants to find funny events. Use this script to help the participants find hidden gems of humor in their lives:

Let's now move on to the second part of the exercise. The circle exercise involved scanning your present landscape for a tangible physical element. The next exercise involves scanning your past for an intangible element.

Here's how you do it. Close your eyes and think of everything that happened last week. Recall all the funny things that happened. Be creative in coming up with laughable events. Pretend that you have a remarkable sense of humor and look at your life for comedy material. Do some creative cheating and put a comic spin on your recent past. Spend 30 seconds doing this.

Give additional instructions. After 30 seconds, ask each participant to pick one of the funniest episodes he or she came up with. Ask everyone to add to the humor if necessary through creative distortion and exaggeration. Encourage participants to keep building on their funny incidents until they cannot contain their laughter. Give the participants another 30 seconds for this exercise.

Share the humor. After 30 seconds, ask participants to pair up and share the funny stories with their partners. Encourage everyone to laugh uproariously at their partners' stories. Roam around the room eavesdropping on different conversations.

Debriefing

Conduct a final debriefing. Share a couple of funnier stories that you overheard on your tour around the room. Continue the discussion with questions such as these:

- *Was it easy for you to discover humorous elements in everyday incidents?*
- *How do you think that the ability to laugh at yourself reduces tension?*
- *Think back on this activity. What are some of the humorous elements in the process?*
- *Who are the people you usually share your funny experiences with? What happens when you do this?*
- *Do you have a favorite comedian? How does this person find humor in everyday incidents?*

 Learning Points

1. Humor can be found in many everyday events.
2. You don't have to be a comedian to make other people laugh.
3. The ability to laugh at yourself is a wonderful quality.

 Variation

Are you a serious person? Instead of asking people to come up with funny incidents, ask the participants to search for happy, inspiring, or positive events.

Jolt 47
What's Measured?

*W**hat is measured (and rewarded) gets done.* Here is a jolt that demonstrates this simple—and powerful—management principle.

 ## Synopsis

Participants answer questions on a handout provided by the facilitator that they all assume is the same. In reality, three different versions of the handout have been circulated, and each version uses a different scoring system that greatly impacts the final outcome.

 ## Purpose

- To explore the relationship between measurement and performance

 ## Training Topic

- Goal focus

 ## Participants

- Three or more
- The best group size for this activity is from fifteen to thirty participants

 ## Time

- 3 minutes for the activity
- 3 to 10 minutes for debriefing

 ## Supplies

- Three different versions of the Performance Improvement handout
- Whistle
- Timer

Preparation

Study the three different handouts used for this activity and make a note of the differences among the scoring systems. Complete the handout tasks as if you were a participant.

Make enough copies of the three different versions of the handout so that an equal number of the different versions will be distributed to the participants.

 Flow

Distribute the handouts. Stress that this is an independent activity and tell the participants not to talk to each other. Pause while the participants read the instructions on the handout.

Conduct the activity. Ask participants to get ready, then blow your whistle and start the timer. Blow your whistle again at the end of 2 minutes and stop the activity.

Ask participants to compute some statistics. Ask each participant to do these three tasks:

1. Count the number of words.
2. Count the number of words that are more than five letters long.
3. Count the number of letters in the longest word.

Locate and congratulate the winners in each category. Find the person with the most total words, the most words that are more than five letters long, and the person with the longest word.

 Debriefing

Explain the differences in the handouts. Tell the participants about the three different versions of the handouts and read the instructions related to the three different scoring systems. Point out that each participant focused on performing the task according to the scoring system specified in the set of instructions given to him or her.

Discuss the impact of misaligned measurement. Discuss how the participants might feel if they were given one type of scoring instructions and the winner was determined by another type.

Discuss similarities in the workplace. Ask the participants how their performance is measured (and rewarded) in their own workplace. Invite them to speculate what would happen if they were measured against different sets of standards.

Discuss the importance of goal setting. Ask the participants to list the advantages of measurable goals and the disadvantages of vague goals in performance measurement.

 Variation

You don't like the phrase "Performance Improvement"? Change it to some other phrase that is more relevant to your participants. Be sure to change the handouts, including the examples.

Field Notes

Using a computer software program, we were able to generate nearly two thousand different words from the letters of *Performance Improvement*. Here are some of the lengthier words: *commemorative, cooperative, cremation, encampment, firmament, impermanent, omnipotence, pantomime, and reinforcement.*

Performance Improvement 1

Your task: Select and rearrange the letters in the words *Performance Improvement* to form different words.

You may use the same letter as many times as it appears in the term. For example, you may use the letter "e" four times in the words you create because it appears four times in *Performance Improvement*. However, you may use the letter "a" only once because it appears only once.

Here are some sample words formed from the letters in Performance Improvement:

ace, epic, print, cement, airport, pretence

How to Win
Time limit: 2 minutes

Generate different words by rearranging the letters in *Performance Improvement*.

Write your words in the lines below.

At the end of 2 minutes, you score 1 **point for each word**.

If your score is the highest, you win the game.

_____

_____

_____

_____

_____

_____

_____

_____

_____

_____

_____

_____

_____

_____

_____

Performance Improvement 2

Your task: Select and rearrange the letters in the words *Performance Improvement* to form different words.

You may use the same letter as many times as it appears in the term. For example, you may use the letter "e" four times in the words you create because it appears four times in *Performance Improvement*. However, you may use the letter "a" only once because it appears only once.

Here are some sample words formed from the letters in Performance Improvement:

ace, epic, print, cement, airport, pretence

How to Win
Time limit: 2 minutes

Remember this important restriction: *Only words that have at least six letters score 1 point.*

Generate as many different words of six or more letters as possible by rearranging the letters in *Performance Improvement*.

At the end of 2 minutes, you will score *1 point for each word that has six letters or more.*

If your score is the highest, you win the game.

_____

_____

_____

_____

_____

_____

_____

_____

_____

_____

_____

_____

_____

_____

_____

Performance Improvement 3

Your task: Select and rearrange the letters in the term *Performance Improvement* to form different words.

You may use the same letter as many times as it appears in the phrase. For example, you may use the letter "e" four times in the words you create because it appears four times in *Performance Improvement*. However, you may use the letter "a" only once because it appears only once.

Here are some sample words formed from the letters in Performance Improvement:

ace, epic, print, cement, airport, pretence

How to Win

Time limit: 2 minutes

Generate long words by rearranging the letters in *Performance Improvement*.

At the end of 2 minutes, we will compare the lengths of words in different lists.

If you have the *longest word, you win the game*. In case of a tie, the person with the most longest words will be the winner.

_____

_____

_____

_____

_____

_____

_____

_____

_____

_____

_____

_____

_____

_____

_____

Jolt 48
Wobegon

The radio host of the popular National Public Radio show *Prairie Home Companion*, Garrison Keillor, claims that all the children in the mythical town of Lake Wobegon are above average. Clearly, this is mathematically impossible to support. But Keillor's underlying social commentary reflects the reality that we all tend to overestimate our own talents, abilities, and accomplishments and underestimate the same qualities in others. This is a jolt that uses this human foible to make its learning points.

 ## Synopsis

Participants individually rate their own listening abilities and the listening skills of others. They compute the average score for both sets and discover this totally human outcome.

 ## Purpose

- To increase our awareness that we tend to overestimate our skills and accomplishments and underestimate the same qualities in others

 ## Training Topics

- Self-image
- Communication
- Critical thinking

 ## Participants

- Five or more
- This activity works best with ten to thirty participants

 ## Time

- 3 minutes for the activity
- 5 to 10 minutes for debriefing

Supplies

- Small pieces of paper
- Pens or pencils
- Flip chart
- Felt-tipped markers

Flow

Obtain personal ratings. Invite participants to rate their behaviors associated with this statement:

I listen very carefully to what the others say.

Ask participants to use this rating scale:

10 = always
 9 = very frequently
 8 = usually
 7 = often
 6 = sometimes
 5 = occasionally
 4 = once in a while
 3 = seldom
 2 = rarely
 1 = never

Ask each participant to anonymously write down the appropriate self-rating number on a small piece of paper, then fold it and give it to you.

Obtain ratings of other people's behavior. Now ask each participant to think of the listening behaviors of other participants (who are attending your session) and rate them using the same rating scale and the same procedure as used in the previous self-rating exercise.

Compute the averages. With the help of the participants, quickly calculate the average value of both the self-rating task and the task of rating of others.

Display the averages. Draw a line like this on a flip-chart page like this:

1——2——3——4——5——6——7——8——9——10

Mark the averages for the self-ratings with an "S" and the "others" ratings with an "O" on the appropriate locations on this line:

Debriefing

It is very likely that you will find the average self-rating to be greater than the average scores for "others." Ask the participants to take a moment to reflect on the implications of this discrepancy.

Jolts! Activities to Wake Up and Engage Your Participants

After a short pause, discuss participants' insights about self-evaluation. Ask probing questions to enable participants to discover our tendency to overestimate ourselves and to underestimate others.

Ask participants to brainstorm different strategies for jointly raising the average listening skills of everyone in the group. Encourage the participants to be accountable for ensuring that the group's improved average reflects new learning gained during this activity.

Variation

Are you interested in exploring other human tendencies and abilities? Instead of asking for estimates of our ability to listen carefully, you might work on other variables such as goal focus, punctuality, accountability, giving feedback, praising others, and participating in discussions.

Jolt 49
Workers and Watchers

In our opinion, Roger Greenaway is a great genius in the area of debriefing (or *reviewing* as he calls it). His work has had a significant impact on the work we do. Here's a jolt that is based on one of Roger's powerful activities.

 ## Synopsis

Blindfolded participants are asked to create a shape on the floor using a length of rope. With the help of observers they learn powerful lessons about working as a team and about effective communication.

 ## Purpose

- To show the power of debriefing

 ## Training Topics

- Teamwork
- Cooperation
- Communication
- Learning

 ## Participants

- Four or more
- The best group size is ten to thirty participants

 ## Time

- 3 minutes for the activity
- 3 to 10 minutes for debriefing

Supplies

- Blindfolds (sleep masks or bandanas), one for each of the participants
- 10-foot piece of rope
- Countdown timer
- Whistle

Preparation

Create an open area so that participants can stand in a circle and move freely around.

Caution

Be careful not to let the blindfolded participants bump into objects or trip or fall down. Remove all obstacles from the open area and encourage the watchers to intervene if any of the blindfolded participants are in any hazardous situation.

Some people do not like to be blindfolded, so give your participants the choice to opt out of being a blindfolded worker and to remain a watcher during both rounds of the activity.

Flow

Brief the participants. Explain that in this activity half of the participants ("workers") will be blindfolded and asked to perform a simple task while the others ("watchers") observe. Explain that later the two groups will switch roles and the newly blindfolded "workers" will be asked to complete a similar task.

Explain the task. Show the length of the rope and explain to the participants that all "workers" will be tasked with laying the length of rope on the floor so that it forms a perfect circle.

Begin the first round. Distribute blindfolds to half of the participants and ask them to put on the blindfolds. Suggest that these workers keep their eyes closed inside the blindfold. Invite the watchers to position themselves around the open area. Place the rope in the hands of two or three blindfolded workers. Ask the workers to begin the task.

Conclude the first round. Set your timer for 1 minute and start it to begin the activity. At the end of 1 minute, blow your whistle and ask all the workers and watchers to stop the activity. Ask the workers to remove their blindfolds. (It does not matter if the task is not completed.)

Debrief the first round. Ask both the workers and the watchers to discuss and answer questions about what happened and what they learned. You will likely have an enthusiastic and spontaneous discussion because the workers will be extremely curious about what the watchers saw. Chime in for the discussion with questions such as: *How does this activity reflect events in your workplace? If you were to do this activity once more, how would you change your behavior?*

Begin the second round. Distribute blindfolds to the participants who were the watchers during the first round. Ask the new workers to put on their blindfolds while the new shift of watchers position themselves around the open area. Place the rope in the hands of a few new workers, as before. Ask these workers to lay the rope on the floor in the shape of a *triangle*.

Conclude the second round. Stop the activity at the end of a minute (even if the task is not completed).

Debriefing

Debrief the second round. Let the workers and observers discuss what happened and answer questions. Encourage all the participants to compare and contrast what happened during the two different rounds.

Ask participants to explore the advantages of debriefing. Encourage the participants to explore the value added by a debriefing discussion.

Debrief the debriefing process. Ask the participants to brainstorm a list of guidelines for improving the effectiveness of debriefing discussions using the core questions below.

Introduce the core debriefing questions. Explain that these questions produce effective results during debriefing discussions:

- *How do you feel about the activity?*
- *What happened during the activity?*
- *What did you learn from the activity?*
- *How does the activity reflect events in your workplace?*
- *What would happen if we changed some of the elements of the activity?*
- *What would you do in the future as a result of the insights from this activity?*

With the help of participants, apply these core questions to this jolt.

Learning Points

1. No one ever sees the complete picture during an activity.
2. Taking time to reflect on an activity helps us learn from experience.
3. Insights gained during an activity vary among those observing it.

Variations

You don't have rope? Ask the blindfolded workers to perform some other task (such as drawing a circle on a flip chart).

You don't have blindfolds? Ask the workers to close their eyes. Alternatively, you may ask the participants to jointly perform a task with their eyes open.

Some participants cheat by peeking? This is a good opportunity for discussing the topic of honesty during the debriefing.

Jolt 50
Your Choice

Customers have more choices than ever. An unhappy customer will likely go to your competitor. This jolt lets your participants play unknowingly the role of the customer and evaluate their own motivation.

 ## Synopsis

Participants choose a writing instrument from an assortment of options in a cup and make decisions similar to those of customers in the real world.

 ## Purpose

- To explore how customers behave and select products

 ## Training Topic

- Customer service

 ## Participants

- One or more
- The best group size for this activity is six to twenty participants

 ## Time

- 3 minutes for the activity
- 10 to 15 minutes for debriefing

 ## Supplies

- Several pencil cups such as empty cups or mugs (You will need one or more cups, depending on the number of participants)
- A variety of writing instruments

Preparation

Place different types of writing instruments in each cup: expensive pens, goofy pens, pens with multi-colored ink, pens without ink, sharpened pencils, blunt pencils, and pencil stubs. Make sure that the number of writing instruments does not exceed the number of participants.

Flow

Brief the participants. Ask participants to put away their own pens and pencils and that they will choose new ones from the cup instead.

Distribute the writing instruments. Tell the participants to select a writing instrument from one of the cups circulating in the room. (Start the cups at different locations in the room.) Ask each participant to take a writing instrument and pass the cup to the next person. When all the pens and pencils are distributed, the activity is over.

Debriefing

Explain that the jolt is over and that the choice each participant made was the point of the activity. Conduct a debriefing discussion using the following questions:

- *What criteria did you use to choose your writing instrument?*
- *Think about the writing instruments that were chosen first. In your opinions, were they the nicer ones?*
- *Think about which writing instruments were chosen last. Were they the broken ones?*
- *What about the goofy looking writing instruments? They looked fun, but perhaps you did not think they would be useful?*
- *What happened when you chose a writing instrument and discovered it didn't work? Did you put it back and look for something better? Why or why not?*
- *How does all of this relate to customer service? Customers want the best product and service and will choose an alternative if they do not like their first choice.*
- *Does your organization consistently give good customer service, or does the quality of customer service diminish, for example, toward the end of the day?*

Learning Points

1. The best products and customer service create customers who are less likely to go to the competition.
2. Customers who feel valued and receive excellent products and customer service are more likely to be repeat customers.
3. Consistently deliver high-quality customer service, even at the end of the day.

Variation

You don't want to use pens? Use a candy dish with a variety of candies and invite participants to choose one each. Include elegantly wrapped candies, common candies, and others that may appear to be half eaten or out of their wrappers.

 ## Field Notes

If fewer participants arrive at your training session than anticipated, remove an appropriate number of the better quality writing instruments. This will force the last participants to choose from the broken or useless writing instruments and therefore emphasize your learning points.

About the Authors

Sivasailam "Thiagi" Thiagarajan is the Resident Mad Scientist at the Thiagi Group. He specializes in designing and facilitating participatory activities for training and other approaches to improving human performance. Thiagi was elected twice, twenty-five years apart, as the president of the International Society for Performance Improvement (ISPI). He has also served four times as the president of the North American Simulation and Gaming Association (NASAGA).

Tracy Tagliati, CPLP, is a Senior Associate at the Thiagi Group. She specializes in designing and delivering training to international clients, developing customized training programs, and facilitating in-house and public workshops. Earlier in her career, Tracy was VP of sales and training at a franchise of Crestcom International and a corporate trainer at Mercury Insurance Group. She is active in ASTD and an executive board member of the North American Simulation and Gaming Association.